The Starfish Chronicles

Rising from Trauma Through Faith, Friendship and Fly Fishing

Sue Kerver

The Starfish Chronicles: Rising from Trauma Through Faith, Friendship and Fly Fishing

ISBN 978-1-961185-93-7 (hardcover)
ISBN 978-1-961185-94-4 (paperback)
ISBN 978-1-961185-95-1 (digital)

Front cover artwork & author photo: Zahrah Bella, The Art Shop *(www.zahrahart.com)*
Author photo: Kelsey Frey *(www.kelseyfreycreative.com)*
Cover design, layout & formatting: Megs Thompson *(www.megswrites.com)*

www.inomniaparatuspublishing.com

Advance Praise for The Starfish Chronicles

"A raw and courageous story told with unflinching honesty, this book pulses with passion and the kind of bravery that gives others permission to rise."

- *Shannon Stroup, Warrior PATHH Guide*

"*The Starfish Chronicles* shares one woman's vulnerable, candid, heartwarming, and heart-wrenching journey, all while reminding us that we aren't alone and that if we are brave enough to share our stories, we can help each other heal."

- *Wendy Dumke, Army Veteran*

"Sue Kerver has reached into the deepest, most painful corners of her soul and brought her truth into the light for the world to see. The bravery required to be this vulnerable is extraordinary, and shines brightly, guiding other women to find their voice, tell their story, and demand to be heard!"

- *Erin McMicheal, Suicide Prevention Specialist*

"A raw, honest reminder that we are never truly alone. *The Starfish Chronicles* reminds us that it's ok to be vulnerable; that's where progress and growth happen. Sue Kerver's experiences show how a person can thrive after sharing their story and remind us that everything worthwhile in life requires hard work."

- *Carrie Fuller, Firefighter*

"*The Starfish Chronicles* celebrates resilience, faith, and the strength of human connection and community. It reminds us that we can do the hard things, finding hope and courage in life's most challenging moments."

- *Lesli Gray, Senior Executive, U.S. Fish and Wildlife Service (Retired)*

"A powerful and unflinching account of trauma and transformation, revealing that what is suppressed inevitably surfaces and that healing unfolds through courage, intuition, and connection. A bold invitation to trust one's deep knowing and embody the Warrior Woman within."

- *Dr. Rebecka Pearson, PhD, Psychological Consultant*

This book contains honest conversations about self-harm, substance abuse, sexual trauma, and the often-uncomfortable tenderness of becoming who we truly are. These stories are shared with care, but not without weight. Please read with care and self-compassion.

For the fierce warriors who came alongside, carrying the torches to illuminate my path through the shadowy places.

For the lionhearts who shepherded me along with steady encouragement, bold courage, and hard-won wisdom.

For those finding their voice in the liminal spaces, where glimmers flicker and Sabotaging Asshats speak too freely.

For anyone who has ever felt unseen, unheard, erased, or unsure, wondering if your story matters.

This is for you. Let's shine together.

Table of Contents

Foreword

When I graduated from University of Texas School of Law in 2001, more women than men were coming out of law schools and joining the legal profession. Now, 25 years later, attrition rates for women in the law remain largely unchanged, and fewer than a quarter of law firm equity partners are women. Statistics are far worse for the armed services—the longer one serves, the fewer women there are, particularly among military leadership. Both the legal profession and military suffer from high rates of depression, anxiety, substance abuse, addiction, and suicide. Both suffer high rates of sexual harassment and assault—which are severely underreported. And both career paths stigmatize such issues to a degree that seeking help—much less overcoming them—can be exceedingly difficult if not career-ending. These struggles are particularly acute for women—we often have to fight twice as hard to achieve half the success of our male peers, and it seems we must sacrifice far more of ourselves in the process.

Why is any of this relevant to *The Starfish Chronicles*—Sue Kerver's beautifully written, painfully insightful, and fearlessly candid memoir recounting her struggles, losses, recoveries, and heroic successes? Because no matter your background, career, or experience, you will find something of yourself in these pages.

Although Sue and I have walked very different professional paths, getting to know her over recent years—and now reading this remarkable memoir—I can't help but feel I have encountered myself from a parallel universe. I met Sue during the COVID years through an organization she and I both serve and love—*Project Healing Waters*, a nonprofit dedicated to helping veterans and men and women in active military service heal through the art of fly fishing. I joined the PHW board in 2018, and some years later found myself on a river in Montana with Sue. And in the years since—whether fishing, working with veterans, or celebrating our 50th birthdays at a Taylor Swift concert in New Orleans—I have come to know Sue as one of the most deeply authentic and driven individuals I've ever had the great fortune to call friend. I've also learned that we share many of the same experiences—including sexual trauma, depression, hard-fought recovery, and professional reinvention. Those experiences, which she shares in this book, are part of who we are—but Sue has done more than recover from them, she has leveraged them into a drive to become the best version of herself. By sharing what she has learned on her path she gives a rare gift to her readers.

This fierce Coast Guard veteran—now fly fishing guide, podcaster, and trauma-informed coach—has accomplished something that, to me, often seems unbearable if not utterly impossible. She has come to know herself deeply and without judgment, and (with that irrepressible initiative of hers) she has summoned the courage to reinvent herself in the image of her best—and wildest—imagining. *The Starfish Chronicles* is so much more than a memoir—it's one of those rare, unflinching recollections of experiences many feel too much shame to share, but without sharing one cannot recover, grow, and thrive. And as I read these pages, I see all the ways in which Sue's experience offers the hope and courage to strive for those dreams that always seemed unrealistic or unattainable. Sue is a hero to many, and she's certainly mine.

- Kendyl Hanks
  Shareholder, Greenberg Traurig, LLP
  Trustee, Project Healing Waters

Author's Note

Throughout the book, I refer to people who made a significant impact on my journey. In some cases, names, personal descriptions and other identifying characteristics have been changed to protect their privacy and ensure confidentiality.

I have not made any changes to the names, or stories, of the women who shared their hearts on the *Two Gals and a Mic* podcast. The full interviews can be found online - https://www.youtube.com/@TwoGalsandaMic/podcasts or by scanning the included QR Code.

I also did not change the name of my husband, Josh, or any of the names or characteristics of my beloved four-legged friends.

I am a Christian, with a strong belief that we are put on earth to do our soul-purpose work, and the path to doing this is guided by the Divine. God and the Divine are important parts of my story. However, I recognize that these terms may be off-putting for some, and that my worldview is one of many. I don't want terminology or my personal philosophies to dissuade you from reading this book. So, I invite you to experience these pages in a way that makes sense for you, bringing in contextual elements from your own belief systems, viewpoints, experiences, and understanding. Inviting diversity and inclusion invites a broader understanding and that is what leads to connection.

Lastly, noting that "sea star" is the preferred scientific term for the echinoderms referenced throughout my story, I made the choice to use starfish, as an ode to both the parable, and the storytelling framework that's resulted from years of self-discovery. So, to all my marine biologist friends, thank you for your grace as I purposefully overlooked the name change which does, indeed, reflect better biological accuracy.

Acknowledgements

To all of you who chose to immerse yourself in these pages, thank you for letting me share my heart with you. I hope my words provide inspiration for you to tell your own stories.

To the powerful Warrior Women who shared your wisdom on *The Two Gals and a Mic* podcast, thank you for your insights, your hearts and your voices. These were invaluable in lighting my path home and fortified my desire to put words to paper.

Thank you to my editor, Mary, and my amazing publisher, Megs, for your instrumental feedback and constant reinforcement. Despite the fear, you pushed me to follow the glimmers and reclaim my voice in a way I didn't realize was possible.

To "Dr. Blackwell," thank you for saving my life and providing me with the very first glimmer that things would, indeed, be ok.

To my counselor, who invited me to stare down those Sabotaging Asshats, thank you for helping me see that my vision is so much more important than selling out to safety.

To all of the people who ever donated your time or treasures to veteran healing programs such as *Project Healing Waters*, *Boulder Crest*, *Camp Southern Ground*, *Warriors and Quiet Waters*, and *The Mission Continues*, thank you. Thank you for investing in me so I may invest in others.

To Sarah and Ken, thank you for helping me survive all the crazy.

And, lastly, to Josh, despite all the words I've written in this manuscript, I could not quite find the right ones to tell you how much you mean to me. Thank you for speaking life into me when I had nothing left and for unequivocally supporting me throughout this amazingly wild journey. I couldn't ask for a better partner, cheerleader and friend.

And a note to my rock steady Meatball…thanks for the love, the licks and the reminder that naps and frequent treats are as important as the grind.

Where I Am From

I am from snow-capped mountain peaks,
From Typhoo tea and Walkers shortbread.
I am from the 1896 Victorian brick manor,
Perched on the corner, spooky, creaking with the desire to be warmed by laughter and love.
I am from summertime Indian paintbrush,
Vibrant, abundant, entreating bees and hummingbirds to share in their copious offerings.
I am from bagpipes and vinyl records,
From (Colonel) Tom and (Lady) Elizabeth.
I'm from spending Saturday morning watching cartoons and Sunday afternoons clipping coupons.
From "Don't play the What-if Game" and "What's for you will not go by you!"
I'm from hand-me-down plaid jumpers and Lenten Stations of the Cross before Friday fish dinners.
I'm from Bethesda, from the French Kervers and Scotland's Glover and Galloway clans.
Yorkshire pudding and asparagus – eaten whole – not with a fork and knife (sorry Mom).
From shadowbox Army medals and black-and-white snapshots of Dad in Korea and Vietnam.
And Mom's closet, brimming with furs, ornate hats and bejeweled dresses.
Offering hours of unsanctioned dress-up entertainment.

Shelves in our downstairs cabinet hold journals, yearbooks and photo albums from decades gone by.
Reminders of where the journey started.
Of the heartaches and triumphs along the way.
A kaleidoscope of memories.
Capturing moments in time, which have shaped five decades of this magnificent life.

What if I were to tell you that where we are from is not as important as where we are going?

It's hard work to talk about our scars. Where I am from is complex, meandering, and less concrete than where I am now. It's full of things I don't want to share, but know I have to, because a leader sacrifices the façade to create opportunities for others to feel safe in exploring their authentic voices.

What if I were to tell you that where I'm from is years, layered with secrets, and not speaking up or sharing my truth, because I was brought up in silos of decorum, of politeness, of following the rules?

What if I were to tell you that where I'm from kept a padlock on my soul, bolted shut, an impenetrable fortress until I found my voice, and myself again, which was the only key that would break it wide open?

What if I were to tell you that where I am from became the foundation, the route, for an inexplicably wild, adventurous, tumultuous journey that brought me back to self?

And, what if I were to tell you that, as I turn the corner on middle age, I am more concerned about "Where I am now," which will become my "Where I am from," someday?

Maybe this is my work now. To trust in the glimmers, as a

Warrior Woman who is no longer afraid. Believing that everything I've learned and amassed along the way is enough to provide an example so others may follow their own paths and know they are not alone.

Why did I stay, walking the hard path? Because giving up felt like an option that wasn't really in alignment. Because of the soft, uneven sand with tides that rush in and rush out, leaving traces of faraway lands that they've carried over miles and miles of oceans. Because I made a promise to God. And He made one to me. That this life is rich. And it's fun.

Because I want to see what's next. They call it 'adventure.' I call it living big, because we are not meant to play small. I stay because this is where I'm meant to be. I stay for faith. For hope, I suppose. I stay because I love wildflowers. And honey. And bees. And the gentle playfulness of a Grizzly sow and her cubs along Alaska's wild riverbanks.

I stay now to tap into my own creative sphere. To continue to find myself so that others may find themselves, too.

When I see my now slowly turning into my then, I see places filled with joy, purpose, and connection because I had the courage to share it here. I now live with freedom and authentic abandon, delighting in the everyday. In the story. In the possibility.

DE LIGHT. OF LIGHT. IN LIGHT. Together.

Introduction

The Starfish Parable

One day, an old man was walking along a beach that was littered with thousands of starfish that had been washed ashore by the high tide. As he walked, he came upon a young girl who was eagerly throwing the starfish back into the ocean, one by one. Puzzled, the man looked at the girl and asked what she was doing. Without looking up from her task, the girl simply replied, "I'm saving these starfish."

The old man chuckled aloud. "There are thousands of starfish and only one of you. What difference can you make?" The girl picked up a starfish, gently tossed it into the water, and, turning to the man, said, "I made a difference to that one!"

(Adapted from "The Star Thrower," by Loren Eiseley, 1978)

Starfish, also known as sea stars, are amazing creatures. Metaphorically, they can symbolize renewal, hope, adaptation, resilience, guidance, healing and rebirth. From a purely biological perspective, these invertebrate echinoderms, which have close ties to their cousins - the sea urchin and the sea cucumber - have figured out ways to adapt to the dangerous marine environments that they often call home.

So much of their life journey aligns with the human experience, especially when we find ourselves creating order from chaos. Much like our life cycles, starfish live in unpredictable environments, where they are in a continual state of stress. As food sources for sharks, sea turtles, crabs, shrimp, lobsters, otters, seagulls, and other predators, uncertainty is probably the only certainty they experience throughout their life spans.

Through the ages, despite threats from sea-dwelling dinosaurs, the ice age, and countless other natural and biological events, these spiny-skinned creatures have survived because they have created and subsequently adopted mechanisms and systems which have allowed them to evolve to meet ever-changing circumstances and make sense of the chaos. They have learned to adapt to dynamic environments, and that has led to their evolution as a species.

Probably the most remarkable adaptation is their incredible capacity to regenerate appendages and, sometimes, their entire bodies, after being exposed to catastrophic situations.

As I reflect on my own journey, there have been times when I've felt like a starfish. I've been that stranded creature on the beach, hoping that somehow, some way, I would figure out how to regenerate and thrive, despite the loss of a marriage, or a business failure or, in my worst-case scenarios, death and complex trauma. So many times, I felt like I'd lost myself to grief, despair, doubt and depression, and that there was no way to move from surviving to thriving.

But, in my journey of discovery, what I found was that my propensity to be resilient, defiant against the odds, and adapt is what allowed me to move from surviving, to arriving, to thriving. When faced with unexpected or unwanted circumstances, I've learned to regenerate my sense of purpose, wellbeing and alignment through a variety of self-care practices and the belief that I could reclaim my voice, follow my intuition and become my own Warrior Woman.

I am a female veteran who experienced sexual trauma and gender disparity while sacrificing myself in service to my country. I am a woman who tried to placate my pain and struggle with self-worth by numbing my shortcomings with alcohol and unreasonable expectations (of myself and others) as I skirted burnout and pretended that my world was not coming unhinged. I am an individual who spent years hiding behind a thin veil of accomplishments, awards and platitudes because I was too ashamed and too scared, to admit that anxiety, depression and Post Traumatic Stress, which resulted from years of complex, compounded trauma, were pushing me closer to falling off an unrecoverable cliff. I wanted to be more than the labels, diagnoses and negative narratives that I carried for decades. I am also a Woman Warrior who decided that I'd had enough, and that I wanted more than to just survive. I wanted to thrive.

As I navigated a healing journey that took me over eight years to walk, I've met myself in exceptionally hard circumstances which required me to evolve from a space of comfort to a place of growth by stretching myself to step into what was well beyond my perceived limitations. I've had to invite alternative viewpoints into my world view and recognize that I was not alone in experiencing pain, heartbreak and tragedy. When I realized that we all are going through this human experience together, it became easier to wave my white flag and ask for help. It also made it easier to try new things when the situation called for different and be open to following intuition and glimmers of understanding, even when the path wasn't entirely clear.

This life journey is as unique to each of us as we are to the world. Throughout my own journey, I've come to understand my innate strength and how powerful choice is in deciding to take the steps, and do the hard work, to heal through difficult and uncertain situations. Like the starfish, I wanted to understand how to overcome setbacks and emerge even stronger. I consider the effort, steadfastness and grit that it takes to grow back from devastation, loss or uncertainty, and I know that we can't do it alone.

On my own path, there were many, many people whom I encountered along the way, sharing love, grace, wisdom, encouragement and light. In these pages, my desire is to pay this forward by offering some of my story and my lessons learned, and then grow a community where stories matter and individuals feel safe to share them because they are embraced by the same authenticity, respect and compassion that was given to me.

I now envision myself as the little girl on the beach, throwing the stranded starfish back into the water, instead of as the starfish, needing to be rescued.

The Starfish Chronicles is my love letter to the world. This is where I get to honor my purpose by helping you consider and excavate your own truths by sharing mine, walk your own paths by providing mine as an example, and give voice to your own stories because, as we discover together, this has the power to create connection and conviction.

In Part I, I share some of the circumstances that brought me to my breaking point. This was not easy material to write, and some may find it triggering. I bluntly speak to the hard topics of suicide, mental health, addiction and sexual trauma. My hope in sharing these pieces of myself is so that you may find ways to dissolve any feelings of isolation, despair, unworthiness and shame, if those are things you are holding onto, and feel encouraged to seek whatever help, support, or lifeline you need so you may step into your full, authentic, beautiful self.

In Part II, I explore what my arriving looked like after I started to reconnect with my voice, listen to, trust, and follow the intuitive glimmers, and fully embrace my Warrior Woman spirit. As a federal employee, I speak candidly about my reaction to the chaos and confusion that emerged in 2025 with a change in administration and a concerted effort to downsize the government workforce. This is not meant to be political or divisive. However, my responses to these factual elements are important in understanding what it looked like for me to finally trust my voice, listen to the glimmers, and live into an embodied Warrior Woman self.

And, in Part III, I explore what it truly means to thrive, including the importance of story because narrative healing and connection are the keystone elements of this work.

I don't want to appear to have crossed some invisible finish line where mental health, or healing, is no longer a factor in my existence. Honestly, I don't think that will ever be my reality. But what I can provide is a living example that there is hope, even in the darkest of places. And, while I acknowledge that it would be helpful to be able to offer a solution to navigate the dark and stormy waters, I can't. As much as I would like to say, "Here are the exact steps on how you may walk your own healing journey," (because that's exactly what I wanted someone to say to me eight years ago), that's not how this works. This is not a self-help book meant to provide answers or shortcuts to enlightenment or some sort of finish line that we are seeking to mark the end of a long and storied journey. (Believe me, if I had that secret sauce, I would have done it years ago.) And, while I am not a doctor, a trained counselor, or mental health provider, what I can offer are lessons I learned as I plodded through the mire. I can also offer the wisdom and insights that some incredible women gifted me, through the *Two Gals and a Mic* podcast. Their stories became beacons of hope that illuminated the way. These women weren't famous. They weren't influencers. They weren't household names. Instead, they were a group of courageous, thoughtful, intelligent, strong women who had persevered through adversity and uncertainty. And their words and insights became the torches that lit my path home.

Your path is uniquely yours to walk, and all the answers and guidance you seek will unfold as they are meant to. What I can tell you, with unequivocal resolve, is that when you do the work to excavate the knowingness that you are gifted, and then trust the process as you implement it, amazing things will happen. How your epic journey unravels will be, in large part, based on your personal choice to push past fear, and your refusal to stay stuck, regardless of your diagnosis, situation or circumstance. So, I encourage you to remain curious and committed to the process.

While I don't have an exact formula to tell you how to walk your own unique path, I can promise that you already have the intuitive compass you need to successfully navigate it.

So, here's to you. You who choose differently. You who trust, even a little bit, to believe that life can be hopeful, gracious with story, with community, with honesty, and with hope. Here's to you for taking a chance on yourself. For creating your own light in the darkness. Magic is happening. You are a one-of-a-kind, beautiful, and wonderful individual. You were made to shine.

Part I:
Surviving

Southern Breeze And Magnolia Trees

"It's funny how we outgrow what we once thought we couldn't live without, and then we fall in love with what we didn't even know we wanted. Life keeps leading us on journeys we would never go on if it were up to us. Don't be afraid. Have faith. Find the lessons. Trust the journey."

-Author Unknown

The cool October nip that marks South Carolina's fall had started to descend on Mount Pleasant, the small beach town where I lived. A pervasive evening chill was settling in, leaving me little choice but to pull out the Patagonia Nano Puff for my sunset beach walk. Harlie, my 7-year-old chocolate lab, was ready to go, so I looked around the tiny garage apartment for her leash, deciding to grab a towel, just in case she got a little over exuberant in the salt water and sand that beckoned as soon as we found our way to the boardwalk. Harlie loved the beach and taking her there for sunset walks became part of my evening routine.

I was unexpectedly pursuing my MBA as a second master's degree, in an accelerated year-long program at the College of Charleston. At 42, going back to school hadn't really been my plan. But neither had divorce.

I loved living four miles from the beach. I loved the simplicity and charm of the whitewashed homes, with the wrap-around porches and metal roofs. Mount Pleasant, a growing suburb of

Charleston, was quaint, ideal, and, well, pleasant. I had found this gem when John Pierre, J.P. for short, my soon-to-be-ex-husband, and I visited the area a year-and-a-half earlier.

We had been married only a few years when we both found ourselves laid off from our oil and gas jobs. In January of 2016, the price of crude oil fell to its lowest price in over a decade and, living in Houston, we both were working in the petroleum industry. Jobs became scarce, and it seemed the entire city was competing for the same few positions that were available for hire. With no sure-footed course in front of us, and a receding economy, our existence had been distilled down to endless "What If" conversations.

"What if we sold our house?" I would ask J.P. "What if we moved to Florida, or North Carolina, or somewhere that's not Houston? What if I go back to school for my PhD while you find a job?" As a veteran, I had the Post 9-11 GI Bill that would pay for schooling, so that last idea seemed like a reasonable stop-gap measure as we tried to figure out our best path forward.

J.P. would placate my ponderings by agreeing to explore some of these options. "Tampa sounds reasonable," he said. "I'll head down there and check it out."

And he did. He spent a week in Florida, and I remained in Texas, certain that he would come back ready and prepared to move.

I was wrong.

As we kicked around new ideas every few weeks, we would settle on a solution and then talk ourselves out of it. The problem was, we never actually made a concrete decision, and would change our trajectory every time the next great idea surfaced, causing an enormous amount of strain in our faltering relationship.

After a few months of being unemployed, the doldrums set in. We were spinning.

"You know," I said to him one afternoon as I was cruising the Internet, "I think we need to have some fun."

"What are you talking about?"

I pointed to the screen that showed pictures of *The Southern Ground Music and Food Festival* in Charleston.

"Sue," J.P. said, "That's in less than a month. You can't be serious."

"Totally serious! I mean, The Zac Brown Band is headlining!" I'd followed them since I was in grad school at the University of Georgia in 2008. "I love them, and they are playing in a place I've always wanted to visit."

"We aren't making any money," he responded. "Probably not very responsible to take off and go on a vacation."

"Yeah, I know," I said, really wanting to make this work. "But I really think we need to take a breather. We could spend some quality time together. Just exhale. Think about it. We could drive, which means we could take Harlie."

I could see his wheels churning and, after a bit more cajoling, I purchased the tickets and we made some loose plans for our next great escapade.

When we showed up at the concert venue three weeks later, the blue bird skies accented a palatable atmosphere that seamlessly juxtaposed southern hospitality with a coastal outdoor music vibe.

"Come on," I said, grabbing J.P. by his t-shirt. "Let's check it out!"

Wisps of cool air permeated my thin pink linen shirt as we walked around the festival grounds, visiting the vodka truck. The fruity-flavored liquid went down smoothly, and the array of options enticed me, so I "tried" more than I should have.

As we walked around the expansive grounds, we stopped at vendor booths to peruse wares that spanned from leather belts with bedazzled buckles to handmade jewelry. And that's when I noticed the queue stacking up in front of one of the vendor tents.

"What's the line for?" I asked J.P. as I looked over to see a crowd of teenagers and college kids waiting patiently for their turn to approach the blue and white tent.

"Dunno," he replied, as we walked over.

The men were all wearing bottoms, some in full pants and some in shorts. All of them had little blue whales dotting the fabric up and down each leg.

"Oh my God!" I exclaimed, the vodka giving me that edge that I mistook as humor. "Whale pants!"

I looked around and realized they were more than a fashion statement. They were part of the uniform that defined this relaxed, coastal vibe. Whale pants, linen shirts, visors, flip flops, and polarized eyewear for the guys. Sundresses, floppy hats, wedge sandals, and trendy sunglasses for the gals.

Giggling, I grabbed J.P. by the arm. "Let's get a beer and find our seats."

With cups in hand, we walked towards the stage, looking for our section so we could finally sit down for a spell.

As we cruised past the line of tents that were closest to the stage, my eyes settled on a large sign, hanging at the entrance of one, that said *CAMP SOUTHERN GROUND*.

"Hey," I said, as I turned towards J.P. "I wanna check this out."

My words were beginning to slur, as we popped into the small space. We were greeted by a woman who was wearing a *Camp*

Southern Ground polo and a big, bright smile.

"Hi!" she said as she closed the gap in between us. "Do you know about *Camp Southern Ground*?"

"No," I answered as I looked at the pictures that littered the tiny tables. There were renderings of an expected near-term expansion on farmland near Fayetteville, Georgia. "I've never heard of it."

"It's Zac's project," she noted, referring to the headliner like he was someone who might pop in for dinner. "We focus on serving youth, and on providing a place for healing and transition for post-9/11 veterans."

My interest was piqued as she handed me a brochure which outlined the vision. I graciously accepted the marketing collateral, pulling myself together and transitioning into a less drunk version of myself for this interaction. Something deep inside told me it was important.

"This looks pretty incredible," I offered.

I hadn't yet grouped myself into the category of the veteran who would need to attend this type of programming, but I was excited to see the efforts being made to help my brothers and sisters.

"Thank you for what you are doing," I said to the nice woman, and then J.P. and I slipped out of the tent to find our seats.

Ironically, eight years after that interaction, I'd recognized that I was exactly the type of veteran who needed that program. I attended Warrior Week, one of *Camp Southern Ground's* keystone programs. That's where I met Megan, the manager of the Warrior Week program, who was passionate about helping veterans in their transformational and well-being journeys. It was during Warrior Week that I walked through a series of assessments and exercises which allowed me to get clear on my values, my strengths, and my purpose, as well as gain meaningful connections.

"The number one thing that I think all veterans need to hear in this country," Megan would later say when I interviewed her on the *Two Gals and a Mic* podcast, which I launched on Veterans Day 2023, with the goal of interviewing 50 women before I turned 50, "[is that] you did serve on behalf of a grateful nation. And you think they don't understand because you have shut yourself up, will not share your stories, and are not giving that nation an opportunity to show their gratitude. Open your mouth, share your story, and connect with someone."

It would take me eight years to understand that story and connection are keys to thriving. But, before I could thrive, I first had to do the hard work and arrive.

The day slipped by with ease as I drank, danced, and drank some more. Like fragments of sand gliding through my nimble fingers, the sun dipped below the horizon and the last set of music was played.

"Time to go," J.P. said as he looked into my glazed eyes.

Hours of day drinking had caught up with me, and my legs were barely able to stay steady as I sloshed my way to the car. I was grateful that J.P. was driving. But he always drove, because he knew that, at the conclusion of any kind of fun-filled event, I wouldn't be able to.

When we woke up in our nondescript motel room the next morning, we were greeted by rays of sunshine peeking through the blinds, and my body felt as crusty as the aged hotel carpet. My head yearned for coffee. I needed something that would extricate the excess alcohol that coursed through my veins from that wild festival day.

"Oh my God," I said, in a barely audible voice as I rolled out of bed. "I feel like crap." My 40-year-old body definitely kept the score.

After showering, we set out, picking a point on Google Maps that wasn't too far from where we were staying. But our trajectory offered the opportunity to explore one of Charleston's surrounding beach communities. We didn't know much about the area, but we did know that, with the little time before the afternoon band kicked things off, we wanted to take in a little sun and salt water. So, we headed south. We'd just crossed the iconic cable-stayed Ravenel Bridge, which was littered with runners and the occasional cyclist on this brisk spring morning. Soon we found ourselves in Mount Pleasant, in search of caffeine and a little pre-concert breakfast.

As we drove a little further, we rounded the corner after crossing a smaller bridge over Shem Creek, and I noticed a sign for a coffee shop coming up on our left.

"There," I said, pointing to a white southern cottage. "Let's go there!"

We parked and walked past the wood sign that was affixed in the ground by two wooden posts to the main door, which was painted coastal blue.

The inside was quaint with chalkboards, reclaimed wood counters and stools, and shiplap walls. My body instantly felt calm as it adapted to the welcoming vibe, and I started to relax and envision what a coastal way of life might feel like.

"I'll have a large vanilla latte and a croissant," I said to the young woman behind the counter.

"And I'll do a large coffee and one of those pastries," J.P. said, as he pointed to the glass that housed a variety of tasty treats.

"Is that all?" she asked. We nodded, paid, and I impatiently grabbed the number, which was affixed to a small metal stand, as the server slid it across the whitewashed countertop.

"You want to go outside?" I asked J.P., pointing to the double French doors that led to an expansive patio and a back garden.

"Sure!"

We made our way outside, taking in the pleasantness of the spring air, combined with a slight coastal breeze, and settled into a picnic table, with a yellow umbrella that poked out of its center. Our spot was a little further away from the gaggle of littles who were gathered around the old Chevy pick-up, which had been converted into a miniature playground for their enjoyment. Still in their church clothes, the kids clamored up the ladder affixed to the side of the truck, to take their turn on the slide, which seemed to be the most popular part of this makeshift play area.

As I looked around at the fairy lights strung up in between magnolia trees, the Adirondack chairs carefully placed around the fire pit, and the families and dogs that just made living here seem so effortless, something in me shifted. It was a moment where this coastal community felt like home. I loved it. And I could envision us living there. Happy. Just like these folks.

"How fun would it be to live here?" I said to J.P. as I sipped the coffee that had finally arrived.

"Are you serious?" he asked. "You know, you'd hate South Carolina."

I rolled my eyes. I was so frustrated with all of the "what ifs" evaporating into thin air, and this felt like just another dream, so close I could almost grasp it, but then it, like all the others, would slip off into oblivion.

On that clear blue South Carolina morning, I felt stuck. Frustrated. Immobile. Sitting there, sipping my coffee and dreaming about the Salt Life, it never occurred to me that, less than a year later, I would be living in a newly-built garage apartment, just a mile from this heavenly haven, tending to a broken heart that fractured because I'd lost this man, who was supposed to be by my side forever.

Despite J.P.'s lackluster response, I knew Mount Pleasant was where I wanted to be. So, shortly after returning to Houston, I applied to attend the College of Charleston's one-year MBA program and received an acceptance letter in the mail soon after.

"J.P.!" I exclaimed excitedly from our little kitchen, "I got in!"

"Got in where?" he asked. I'd applied for so many graduate programs, it was hard to keep track of what I was celebrating.

"College of Charleston," I said in an exasperated tone. "Let's do this! Let's make a move. We can live in Mount Pleasant," I added, thinking about that quaint beach town where we had found solace beneath the magnolia trees.

"Yeah, I don't think so," he responded.

"Why not?"

"Because it doesn't make sense. And, besides, you really would hate living there. It's hot and South Carolina isn't as progressive as you think."

End. Of. Discussion.

My frustration mounted. I was at the end of my thinly connected tether, tired of being told "no" when all I was looking for was a "yes." So, in a defiant move, where my anger got the better of my judgement, I applied for a corporate gig in San Diego, knowing that California was one of the few places J.P. absolutely would not go.

I got a call a few weeks later, with an invitation for an in-person interview.

"They want me to fly out to San Diego," I said to J.P. as soon as I learned I'd advanced to the final round. The first few interview rounds had gone well, so this should have been exciting news.

"Are you going to go?" he asked.

"I don't know. What do you think?"

"I think you should," he said. "It's a job."

It *was* a job, but it was also in a place where J.P. wouldn't live. So, nothing about the decision to accept that invitation felt settled. Yet, I did it anyway. I ignored that feeling as I shoved it deep down and replaced it with all the reasons why I felt this made sense. If I'd listened to my inner-knowing and trusted myself enough to follow the glimmers, maybe, that wouldn't have been the nail in our marriage coffin. But I made my choice, and that choice had consequences.

When the cabin door shut, and the pilot announced we were ready to take off, my calm demeanor stepped aside so a full-blown panic attack could emerge. Gripping my seat, I felt the inexplicable need to run, to escape. But I was trapped, with nowhere to go, as the plane backed out of the gate and made its way to the tarmac.

I hadn't had a panic attack in over a decade, and, as I learned more about the autonomic nervous system years later, I would come to understand that my sympathetic system had been triggered, and, instead of being in homeostasis, I was in a fight or flight response.

"*Breath Sue*," I told myself, as the plane took to the air. "*B-R-E-A-T-H-E.*"

I closed my eyes and willed myself into a fitful slumber, arriving in San Diego a few hours later. I had no time to process what had happened, and, instead, grabbed the car, plugged the address into my phone, and headed directly to the interview.

I wasn't ready to trust my intuition. And, instead of recognizing that the excessive anxiety was a response to my rational and emotional brains being in conflict over this decision, I chalked the panic attack up to fear of flying. I hadn't yet found a way to amalgamate the emotional and rational parts of my brain to find common ground, so I didn't make choices based on Wisdom. And that didn't serve me well at all. I let that singular incident stymie my desire to fly and, for years after, I had to follow a meditative ritual to be able to make it through a travel day.

A month later, I signed the offer letter, silently acknowledging that my choice to move to San Diego was also a choice to leave J.P.

"I can't do this anymore," he said as he handed me the plain manila envelope, a few months later, at the conclusion of his first and only trip down to see me. No pomp or circumstance. No fighting for a relationship that had run its course. Just a decision his heart had made, that my heart would have to learn to adapt to.

It didn't take me long to leave the job in San Diego and head to Charleston. I'd been able to defer my admission to the MBA program, and I yearned for a fresh start. Part of me lived with false hope that maybe leaving California would be a way for J.P. and me to reconcile our differences. And that false hope eventually showed me that, once again, I was wrong.

I had been married once before and was sure that this second time around would be forever. J.P. and I seemed like a great match. Yet, here I was, less than two years after saying our vows, reeling from a divorce that left me hollow. There was a trail of losses littering my path. I'd lost J.P. I'd lost my job. I'd lost myself. And I'd lost my way. I was slowly coming to terms with the fact that my actions, and just as equally my inactions, contributed towards total destruction.

The Reckoning

"The Good Road and the Road of Difficulties you have made me cross; and where they cross, the place is holy."
– Black Elk

As Harlie and I walked the beach, I watched the sky light up in deep red and orange hues, the sun dipping closer towards the Atlantic Ocean's beckoning waters. My toes sunk deeper into the wet sand, and I could feel my brokenness expanding. I ached to release the damaged, unworthy and discarded feelings, hoping they would seep out through my feet and be washed away with the receding tide. The notions of aloneness and desperation lingered, making me believe I would never feel normal, I would never again experience joy, and that happiness was, indeed, just an illusion.

I watched the ocean deposit traces of faraway places as the breaking waves crested, pushing its waters towards the sand dunes. The tide crept up to the bank, before receding back into the abyss, taking with it remnants of the island that would become fodder for someone else's beach walk. As the waters churned, I watched my footprints disappear and sand fill in the holes that my feet had just made. It wasn't that I felt sad. I wasn't despondent or depressed. I was just flatlined. The truth is, I felt all those emotions so regularly, I didn't recognize them as warning signals. This lingering melancholy had become my new normal.

Since making the choice to leave San Diego and move to

Charleston, I'd become accustomed to days being peppered with a rollercoaster of anxiety, followed by sweeping waves of depression, with unexpected instances of intense panic. Every day was a game of Russian roulette, where I wondered which emotions would show up, and when they would overtake my peace. I'd come to rely on unpredictability being my new normal, and, coupled with the stress of trying to complete an MBA in a year, I was flailing. I spent numerous hours in talk therapy, but nothing seemed to make a difference. To my own detriment, instead of processing these reactions in healthy ways, I internalized them, feeding the narratives that I'd created which told me, in unceasing tapes running through my head, that I was *Broken, Unworthy, Damaged* and, the peskiest of all, *Not Good Enough*. These false stories, which I adopted at a very early age, taunted me as I tried to remain in control in my personal and professional lives.

I was a high-performing adult who had a history of being strong and capable. A leader. Falling apart just wasn't an option because it was my job to hold everyone and everything together. So, being honest or open, especially outside of a therapist's office, and especially about my mental health struggles, was not something I was ready to do. Even if I was, I wasn't sure how to feel safe, supported or validated in speaking my truth. So, I stayed silent.

But behind closed doors, I talked to countless doctors, who all seemed to be working from the same outdated checklist. "Just take these anti-depressants," some would say. So, I did. And, for a long time, I lived with the veiled illusion that the combination of pills and weekly counseling would make everything better. But, despite my best efforts, I suffered in silence because I was not equipped with the proper community, support and permission to make headway in healing.

I continued to spiral.

I felt alone and utterly discounted.

I was circling a drain that was ready to engulf me, begging me to finally give up.

A few months earlier, on a bright June morning, I left the Galveston County Courthouse parking lot with finalized divorce papers in hand. J.P.'s last words… "I still love you" … echoed in my ears. I drove north, until I found a Texas beachline where I could walk. One step. One breath. One foot in front of the other. I kept moving until the bottoms of my feet were raw and bleeding, until I had exhausted my reserve of tears and darkness set in. I didn't have an answer to the pain that shattered my heart. It was so broken, I figured it was impossible for it to ever heal.

Now as I walked a different beach with Harlie, I again wondered if life would ever get better. Looking down, I saw my footprints, and it reminded me of the poem, *Footprints in the Sand*, by Mary Stevenson, that we distributed at Mom's funeral.

With an explicit promise that we are carried during times of trouble and uncertainty, I wondered why I was still plodding along, on my own, without any support. So, for the hundredth millionth time, I called out, pleading for my Creator to help me understand how I had ended up here, discouraged, uncertain and alone.

"Why God?" I asked, as I looked up into a sky that was starting to darken. "Am I EVER going to feel normal? I just can't…"

I didn't hear God's voice and, instead, heard the lapping of the waves, the call of the seagulls and the occasional sound of a ship's whistle as deep draft vessels, shrimp boats and recreational skiffs navigated the channel that connected the safer parts of the inland harbors with the wilds of the Atlantic Ocean. I wasn't even sure if He wanted to hear from a broken, worthless, shell of a woman.

It would take me a while to recognize that my God language, that language of intuition, didn't come in spoken form. It came as glimmers. My intuitive love language was the knowingness that burned deep in my belly and directed my path as my own North Star. But I wasn't yet tuned into that and certainly didn't know how to speak that dialect.

Harlie and I had walked our two miles, reaching our turn-around point to head back to the entrance just as the sun was dipping below the horizon. With red, orange and pink tones filling the twilight sky, I paused to take the prerequisite selfie pictures so I could post them later to Facebook. Despite the internal turmoil, my external social media feed looked like I was living my best life. The reality was, I had been on a downhill trajectory for a long time and, unbeknownst to me, this evening would be when my trainwreck would finally get me to the proverbial end-of-the-line.

When Harlie and I made it back to the beach entrance, we walked slowly down the boardwalk, towards my silver 4-Runner. I breathed deeply, glancing back over my shoulder, taking in the waving sea oats, darkening sand, and inky blue sky one last time. It was breathtaking, mesmerizing, and should have been a storybook scene that elicited calm and healing. Yet, all I felt was a deep-seated fatigue that had settled into my heart and my soul. It wasn't burnout or just being tired. It was a feeling of finality.

When I got home, as part of my post-beach ritual, I settled into the white canvas loveseat next to the kitchen, opened a bottle of wine, and began to scroll through the online dating sites. Sometimes I would engage in wine-infused conversations with potential suitors and often realized, the following day, that many of these text messaging strings went sideways after my second or third glass of Cabernet.

Both of my parents were alcoholics, and drinking was commonplace in our household. Growing up, I was a good student, a rule-follower, the kid who never got in trouble. I craved a structured environment because it brought order to the chaos. Now I was craving that same structure and looking for someone who could help provide it.

The first bottle of wine went down quickly. I opened a second, fully engaged in a text messaging conversation with Reilly, a man who had also spent his life in service. I met Reilly a few months earlier and found that he loved good food, great wine and dogs. Our first date had been fun, and a little over the top. What started with dinner and a few drinks had ended the next morning with an intense hangover, my inability to finish breakfast at the quaint beach dive that was famous for their fare, and the need for rehydration that only an IV's drip could provide. Despite the messiness of our first encounter, we continued to see one another, building a romantic connection that, in reality, my broken heart wasn't ready for.

But that night, as the texts and emojis flew, I guzzled wine, barely paying attention to the dating drama that was emerging on the latest edition of *The Bachelor*. Despite being fully ensconced in a text conversation with Reilly, I felt alone. But my aloneness wasn't a superficial ache. It was the deep-seeded loneliness that comes when purpose and passion have vacated your soul. The kind of isolation that permeates your being with whispers of despair, making you believe that you will always, and forever, be without the reason that we all need as fuel to propel us through the hardest of times.

I sat on that couch, completely disconnected. I was disconnected from the text conversation, from myself, from my life, and from that Warrior Woman whom I once had been.

Eventually, I put the phone down and stumbled over to the tiny kitchen, which was just steps away from that white canvas-covered loveseat where I'd just been sitting. I opened a drawer near the sink and pulled out a variety of large knives, placing them on the coffee table in front of the TV. I picked them up, one by one, staring at the shiny metal weapons. Tiny fragments of light bounced off their stainless-steel edges, a beautiful dance of colors and prisms that bounded off the sharp, scary, intense blades. After watching the reflective dance for a few minutes, I lost interest and, making my way back to the kitchen, put the knives down on the granite counter next to the refrigerator. I stumbled to the bathroom and opened the medicine cabinet. I stared at the orange pill bottles which lined the second shelf. For years, I had tried, unsuccessfully, to onboard a variety of psychotropics to deal with the depression and anxiety. And, with each new attempt, side effects would worsen, which created a visceral dislike of taking medications. So, my pharmaceutical options were pretty limited.

"*Which one of these bottles*," I silently wondered, "*would make all of this go away?*"

Suicide hadn't been part of my life plan. I knew that, with almost everything in life, I could make a different decision if the original one didn't pan out. But, with this singular action, once executed, there was no turning back. Final meant final.

As I stared at the couple of plastic bottles that took up space on the bottom shelf of the medicine cabinet, I didn't see another way out. I was tired, exhausted by the constant feelings of overwhelm and worthlessness that crept into so many of my waking moments. I wanted to share my grief and pain, but I didn't know how to safely do that. And, I was too ashamed to speak the truth about the memories that plagued me. I didn't want to give voice to the ghosts that haunted me, from when I'd grown up in a tumultuous household, from when I'd been a Peace Corps volunteer in Africa and witnessed the atrocities of gender disparity in action. From when I'd served in the Coast Guard and was on the front lines of pulling women, children, babies out of stinking fish holds as their rickety vessels threatened to succumb to Davy Jones' Locker.

Shortly after finishing college, I moved to Areka, Ethiopia, where, as a Peace Corps volunteer, I lived in a mud hut and taught English at a high school in a rural southern village. Day after day, I would scan my overcrowded classrooms, and look into the haunted eyes of young men, and a few young women, who were fighting for survival because they'd been born into abject poverty.

As I stared at the pill bottles, I thought about the faces of the young women whom I met during my time in Africa. There was the young woman whom I paid to bring water from the river. Another whom I paid to wash my clothes. And there were the little girls who lived next door, greeting me every day with big eyes and bright smiles, as they played in the dirt outside my front door, nonplussed by their soiled and torn shirts, or the flies that they would occasionally swat from the corners of their mucus-caked eyes.

I picked up one of the orange bottles and inspected the label. My eyes couldn't focus on the tiny print, and my mind wandered again, thinking about all the sexual trauma I'd navigated over the years. There was the incident at a formative age, more during my high school years when I had to thwart the uninvited advances of my mom's male adult "friends" and even more when I served in the Coast Guard.

I don't doubt that Mom loved us and, as my siblings and I grew into our adult years, she worked hard to make amends for the rocky relationships that she had forged with us. During my childhood, I'm not sure that she knew how to fully express love. So, without other women to guide me, I didn't understand what it should look like to show up in my feminine energy, or how it would feel if I was both soft and compassionate, bold and assertive.

My dad, on the other hand, was a highly educated man who took pride in his work. Despite a 20-year career in the Army, he didn't talk much about his military experiences. He had been deployed to Korea and Vietnam as a Public Affairs Officer and, later, spent years at the Pentagon working for high-level officials Without verbalizing it, Dad made it clear that assertiveness and, at times, curtness, were critical elements of establishing the command presence that would be needed to navigate through life. He had a curmudgeonly demeanor and could be downright obstinate when he'd had too much to drink. But he could also be fiercely protective, showing love through acts of service instead of words of affirmation. To me, he was the guy who loved to watch the Cleveland Browns on Sunday afternoons, who could make an exceptional Yorkshire pudding, and whom I wanted to impress more than anyone. I wanted to be just like Dad – smart, financially solvent, well-respected and making an impact in the world.

Yet, here I was, in my bathroom, willing the power of my

destiny to these plastic pill bottles with childproof caps.

I had been trained, first from my father, and later in the Coast Guard, to push the fear down, keep the bad bottled up, and forge forward. I routinely experienced cognitive dissonance between who I authentically was and how I was expected to show up. There was no room for emotion, and I'd been taught that vulnerability was not how leaders should position themselves. I didn't want to let anyone know that I was suffering because I honestly believed that would make me look weak. And, moving forward showed the world I was strong, capable and resilient.

As a woman who had grown up with the expectations of high achievement and success, and who later lived in professional worlds where being aggressive and assertive were the only way to gain a seat at the table, I believed that being a Warrior meant sacrificing the softer, more feminine sides of me. What I didn't understand yet was that embracing my feminine energy was the only way I'd be able to reconnect with my Warrior Woman. And, in the reconnection, I would find the balance between these two sides of self.

As I picked up each bottle, the tiniest glimmer began to take shape, deep in my belly. It started as an inkling, just a small knowingness, and then grew into a warmer urging, asking me desperately to reconsider my decision. That whisper promised that, if I would just trust and endure, there was something better for me, something that I was put on earth to do, something that would give me purpose.

"*Sure,*" I muttered to myself as I put the bottles back on the shelf and pushed the medicine cabinet door closed. "*Sure, there is.*"

I stumbled from the bathroom to the bedroom and collapsed

into the mattress. "God," I cried out in earnestness again, "I can't keep doing this. If this is the way it's going to be, just don't let me wake up. It's just too much. Please let me be done."

Some prayers really are better left unanswered.

The next morning, my eyes fluttered open, and I stared at the ceiling in a hazy, hung-over fog. As a highly functioning alcoholic, I was used to the morning doldrums, where the only way to release the fatigue and fog was to over caffeinate and over stimulate. It was Friday, and I had an important round-table discussion I needed to attend for my graduate work. I was gearing up for the weekend, expecting to run the James Island Connector 10K and then meet some girlfriends at the corn maze and grab drinks afterwards.

Something about this morning felt different. Heavy. Real. I couldn't will myself to push through the hangover and forge ahead with my day. So, I stared at the ceiling and ran through the series of events from the evening before. I remembered the kitchen knives, the pills, my ghosts and the ambiguity with which I had considered my predicament.

This morning, I had no choice but to accept that I was in crisis.

I finally found the courage to get out of bed and into the shower. The warm water knocked off the cobwebs and once dressed, I headed to the kitchen to put on a pot of coffee. Out of habit, I carried my phone in my left hand, and, before I knew what I was actually doing, my right hand started dialing.

"You've reached the veteran's hotline," the recorded voice said. "Press one if you are in crisis. Press two…"

My finger had already hit the number one on the screen pad.

I heard the elevator music that indicated I was on hold, waiting to be connected to a live person. "*FUUUCK,*" I screamed into my empty kitchen. "*Who puts a suicidal veteran on hold?*"

Finally, a female's voice replaced the enervating instrumental tones.

"This is the Veterans Crisis Line," she said. "Are you in crisis?"

My inside voice was vehemently throwing more F-bombs. *"Should I hang up?"* I wondered, looking at that solid red button that would end the phone call. I hadn't even had my first cup of coffee and already the day was unraveling at record speed.

I knew I couldn't hang up because I couldn't postpone the inevitable any longer. I was in crisis but too scared to breathe the words out loud. There was a reason my fingers had dialed the numbcr and thc voicc at the other end of the line was my best option if I wanted to find an actual solution to my growing angst.

So, instead of giving into fear that would lead me down an easier road, I took a breath, steeled myself, and simply answered, "Yes."

That was the first time I audibly admitted the magnitude of my situation. I felt like a failure. I should have been able to handle this, but I knew that I couldn't. I was defeated.

That one-word admission led to a short conversation where I was advised that a care provider from Charleston's VA hospital would call me back shortly. And that was that.

Even though I didn't recognize it at the time, this phone call was a defining moment. One of the most valuable lessons I would learn, which originated with that phone call, was that I was deserving, I could ask for what I needed, and I had the authority to advocate for myself.

Yellow Paper Gowns

"Life is amazing. And then it's awful. And then it's amazing again. And in between the amazing and the awful, it's ordinary and mundane and routine. Breathe in the amazing, hold on through the awful, and relax and exhale during the ordinary. That's just living a heartbreaking, soul-healing, amazing, awful, ordinary life. And it's breathtakingly beautiful."

- L.R. Knost

After hanging up the phone, I pulled the half-and-half out of the fridge and turned my attention back to the coffee pot that teemed with the promise of a much-needed boost. Then I dressed in a light fall sweater, knee-high brown boots and a scarf dripping with oranges and creams. Somehow, it felt important to show up looking pulled together, even though my world was fracturing into a million tiny pieces.

I strode through the Charleston VA hospital's parking lot a bit later, authoritative and purposefully, as if it were any other Friday and I had control of the entire afternoon.

As I entered the sliding glass doors, I could feel the buzz of a facility awash with activity. Veterans in wheelchairs and walkers littered the hallways. Caretakers strolled alongside. Hospital staff moved with purpose, calling patients from waiting rooms at their scheduled appointment times and the occasional overhead announcement played on the speakers.

My first steps through those sliding glass doors led me into the Hall of Heroes. My boots clicked on the tiled floor as I walked down the fluorescent-lit corridor which was lined with portraits of veterans whose faces had stories to tell. I could feel their eyes burn into my back as I passed each uniformed member, representing all services, races and ages.

Years ago, when I lived abroad in Paris as an exchange student for a single semester, I visited the Louvre and spent hours studying the Mona Lisa. Her eyes were haunting, with an uncanny way of following my every action, my every twitch, my every breath.

But she didn't judge. She simply noticed. And watched. As I moved down the Hall of Heroes, I felt that same phenomenon, as if I was again being watched. But this time, I was also being judged as I made my way deeper into the hospital's belly. The veterans on those walls, with their steely eyes and grizzled faces, were telling me that I should have been able to handle my shit. I should have been stronger. And harder. And more capable. I was better than this. What they didn't know was that, despite my external façade, my internal essence had cracked.

As I came to the end of the Hall of Heroes, I found the elevators and hit the "up" button. I took a sharp breath in, hoping no one would board the car with me. It's not that I minded company. I just didn't want anyone to make the connection that I was headed to floor five, because one only went to floor five to see the executives or the psychiatrists.

The elevator ride seemed excruciatingly long, and when the car finally arrived at the fifth floor, I realized I was alone in the elevator. Stepping out into the corridor, I immediately looked for signage to direct me where to go. I transited a maze of hallways until I found the check-in window, which was occupied by another patient. So, I stood in line, patiently waiting until it was my turn. I felt exposed, and embarrassment crept in. I pulled out my phone and numbly opened Facebook, deciding to hide in plain sight, but under the cover of scrolling through everyone else's perfect lives.

"Last name and last four of your social?" The male voice roused me from my bubble as I looked up to find the window had finally opened.

"Kerver, with a K," I said, and then offered the rest of the information.

"You're all checked in. Have a seat and someone will be with you shortly."

Turning my back to the clerk, I scanned the small waiting room and looked for a nondescript seat where I could hunker down until my name was called. The faint combination of must and body odor hit my nostrils as I walked past other veterans who were flipping through magazines, scrolling through phones, or absently staring at the television that blared in the corner.

I sat down in a seat near the windows and waited. My boots distractedly tapped the concrete squares in the flooring as I heard the repetitive sound of the check-in window slide open and closed. Open and closed. Sealing itself with a click on every rotation.

The sound lulled me into a catatonic state until I was aroused back to the waiting room's white walls when I heard someone call out "Kerver!"

I looked up and noticed an older woman, with a welcoming smile and clipboard, scanning the waiting room to see who would answer. I stood up and shuffled towards her, meeting her smile with a frown as she led me through an ominous set of double doors, down another brightly lit corridor, around a corner and to her office. Stopping briefly to turn the metal knob, she pushed open her door, revealing a space lit from the afternoon sun that was pouring in through the picture window behind her tiny desk. I took a seat in the cushy chair, poised to the left of her desk, and, as the office door closed behind us, let out a long sigh.

I hadn't fully exhaled before streams of tears began rolling down my face. I struggled to understand how, once a strong, independent, accomplished, professional woman, I was now reduced to rubble. Here I sat, sobbing uncontrollably, in this office, in this predicament, on this lazy fall afternoon, and we hadn't even had a chance to get started.

"Sue," she said, "I'm Dr. Blackwell. I understand you're having some…trouble." She paused on that last word, letting it sink in, and then continued gently. "What's going on?"

I couldn't find the words to adequately express what I was feeling. So, I wept. I wept for the situation, for the woman I once was, for all of the parts of me which no longer felt connected, or tethered, or important. I cried for my inner child who had felt unworthy and abandoned for so long, for the dreams I had lost or been too scared to pursue, for the shell of the person whom I had slowly become, and for the uncertainty that surrounded all of it.

With her compassionate smile and slow tone, Dr. Blackwell continued to question me, now focused less on the suicidal ideation that had brought me here in the first place and more on next steps.

"Sue," she started, as she slowly moved her chair from behind her desk to directly in front of me. She was closing in, her knees almost touching mine as she leaned in. "Can you keep yourself safe over the weekend?" Her eyes met mine directly, and my heart stopped.

It seemed like an easy question.

"*Just say yes*," I told myself. "*Leave the office, go home and get back to normal. Forget about all of this.*"

I was a pro at stuffing the hurt. I had done that for decades. But truth be told, it was a big deal. A very big deal. And, this time, I just couldn't. After all, I was the one who had reached out for help, so what sense would it have made to give into the fear, disappointment and shame and let those things dictate next steps?

I dug myself firmer in the seat of the chair, my grip tightening on its arms. "I'm not sure," I admitted, locking eyes with Dr. Blackwell, allowing vulnerability to enter the space between us.

"Do you have a safety plan?" Dr. Blackwell inquired. "Or should we make one?"

I had never even heard of a safety plan. I never had a reason to make, or have one, so I wasn't sure what it entailed, and less sure of what I would do with it if I was sent home to face the weekend alone.

"No," I said simply. "I suppose we need to make one."

"Do you think you could keep yourself safe if we did make one?" she countered.

"I…" stopping short of answering fully, I took another breath to consider. "I don't know."

"*HOW*?" I asked myself. "*How am I sitting here, so indecisive, about the ONE THING I need to be sure about?*"

Confirming, in that answer, that I was a risk to myself, Dr. Blackwell suggested that I consider voluntarily admitting myself to the hospital for the weekend.

"It would just be for a couple of days," she assured me. "Until we can figure out a plan on how you can keep yourself safe."

"*Wait, what? No. No. NO! What will I do with Harlie? And what about my 10K run?!*" The anxious thoughts ping-ponged around in my head, never taking shape in my mouth. "*Oh my God*" I thought, "*Is she seriously asking me if I want to commit myself to a psych ward?*"

My nonverbal response cued her to speak again. "Sue, we need to make a decision. Do you have someone we can phone who may help you do that?"

I nodded and pulled out my cell phone. I opened my contacts, found my sister's number and placed the call.

When Sarah picked up, sobs overtook my throat, and I was barely able to say hello.

"Sue, what's happening? What's going on?" Her tenor raised an octave as she expressed the last question with concern.

My breath caught, and I just couldn't find the words. It was all I could do to just sit in the chair, breathing heavily, as my world continued to collapse.

"Hi. I'm Dr. Blackwell," she interjected. "Sue is here with me, at the VA hospital. She came in today because of her concern that she was going to hurt herself and is uncertain if she is able to keep herself safe over the weekend."

A heaviness filled the air as the gravity of the situation filled the negative spaces.

"We've talked a bit and we are thinking that it could be a good idea to admit her to the hospital for the weekend, until we can figure out a plan."

Hearing those words felt like an anvil had landed on my head, crushing my entire body from the skull down. I wondered if this was me hitting rock-bottom.

After a bit more discussion about what this would mean, and what would happen once I was released, I finally conceded to voluntarily checking myself in.

"I'll do it," I said. After all, it was only for the weekend, and Sarah had promised to call Reilly to help with Harlie's care.

Hanging up the phone, Dr. Blackwell typed a few things into the computer and, a few minutes later, she escorted me out of her office.

"This is a better route," she said as we entered the back stairway that led directly to the emergency room on the first floor. "Less crowded."

I appreciated her discretion. And, despite the embarrassment and shame of it all, I felt, for the first time since this experience began, that someone had my back.

Arriving in the emergency room, Dr. Blackwell handed me off to the charge nurse for in-processing. "Good luck, Sue," she said and then paused slightly, looking me directly in my swollen eyes. "You're going to be ok." And then she turned and walked away.

I exhaled as the nurse looked through my chart, citing in on the notes Dr. Blackwell had entered. She then escorted me to a small room which was sheltered from the business of the ER's main area. She handed me off to two male nurses, one of whom offered me a relatively see-through yellow paper hospital gown and, with an air of indifference, asked me to change into it.

"You'll need to remove your underwire bra. You can put all of your clothes and things here," he instructed, pointing at a small plastic bag that was sitting on the chair.

I shut the door, complied with the request and then laid down on the naked bed in the stark hospital room, the yellow paper gown crinkling beneath my physical and emotional weight. One of the male nurses knocked on the door to assess my status and, able to ascertain that I was fully, although barely clothed, left the door in an open position so they could maintain the mandatory suicide watch.

As I laid on the bed, and stared at the second ceiling of the day, I listened to the hushed tones of the two male nurses, engaged in a pretty lengthy discourse. As they sat at the nurse's station, just outside the door, I could distinguish just enough dialogue to figure out they were discussing my next steps.

"Are you cold?" one finally asked as he peeked in the room. "I can get you a blanket."

I glanced down at my semi-transparent yellow paper gown and nodded.

He brought me a thin, overly starched cotton blanket, and I draped it over the paper gown, trying to restore the dignity that had been erased when my undergarments landed in the nearby plastic bag.

Minutes continued to tick by but, with no windows or a clock, it was hard to tell how much time had passed. My mind circled the endless possibilities of what might come next, and I created story after catastrophized story of what this all would mean.

"Ms. Kerver," one of the nurses said, interrupting my rumination, "we will need to get a urine sample so we can do a pregnancy test."

It didn't occur to me that a pregnancy test was an odd thing to ask for in this situation. But I didn't argue and headed down the hall to the nearby restroom, hoping no one could see through the thin yellow paper that crunched and crackled with every movement I made.

I would later review those hospital notes and realize that the "pregnancy" test was actually a drug test. And the question I'd struggle with, well after the fact, wasn't why they tested me for these things, but, rather, why they withheld the truth of what they were doing.

When I returned to my room, one of the male nurses advised that I would have to wait a bit longer. “We don’t have any open beds here at the VA to accommodate a female,” he said. “So, we are going to have to transfer you to a mental health inpatient facility across town.”

“How long is that going to take?” I asked. He shrugged his shoulders, not having much more information than what he already provided.

“Well, if I have to continue to wait, can I at least use my phone?”

The two looked at one another, as if no one wanted to make that decision, and it dawned on me much later that I was likely asking them to breach protocol with this simple request.

“Sure,” one finally said, and handed me my iPhone.

I laid back down on the bed, not sure who to call or what to say. So, I texted Sarah and offered her a status update. Then I texted Reilly to check on Harlie and, having exhausted the list of people whom I trusted with this info, I closed my eyes.

As I sprawled out on the hospital bed, minutes turned into hours. The orderlies continued hushed conversations just beyond the threshold of my room’s open door. Lying there, mostly naked under my see-through yellow paper gown and hospital blanket, I stewed.

“*Why*,” I wondered, as I lay there and thought about things, “*has no one thought to ask me what it would take for me to feel safe*?"

Eight years later, I would go through a trauma-informed coaching program, and learn how the brain processes and integrates acute, chronic, complex and generational trauma. In this nondescript emergency waiting room, my subconscious brain was registering the entire experience as a series of traumatic microaggressions that would later fuse to my overall sexual trauma story. Ironically, I was in that little room because I didn't feel like I could keep myself safe. Yet, in the yellow paper gown, I was put in a position where I didn't feel like others could keep me safe either.

As I studied trauma years later, I would come to realize that part of the reason I felt emotionally raw, vulnerable, weak and unsafe was because I did not feel equipped or empowered to speak up on behalf of my highest self. I had been silenced for so long, I had lost my voice.

I could have asked for a sports bra. Or a female nurse. Or a cloth gown that didn't leave me feeling so exposed. But I'd grown up in systems where compliance was imperative to mission completion, and I felt that, even in this uncomfortable situation, the care team knew best. So, I didn't use my voice to ask for what I needed. And what I really needed was a paradigm shift where my voice was valued and I had the courage to use it.

In this space of vulnerability, I was unconsciously starting to redefine my view of what it meant to be a hero and, more importantly, a Warrior. This was no longer about the external accolades, like those written below all the hero portraits I'd walked by on my way to the elevator. Instead, the shift to connecting with my Warrior Woman meant speaking up and advocating for myself and, eventually, others. It meant learning to listen to my intuitive love language. And it meant recognizing that I couldn't do everything by myself.

I would need to create a support system, filled with other trusted women, and men, whom I could rely on in times like these.

It also meant that I would have to create a change that would set my Warrior Woman free from the chains and constraints society, and my own background and experiences, had placed on Her. This shift – and what I consider to be the start of my healing journey – ignited a spark deep inside my spirit. It set ablaze an authoritative fire of Divine energy within my soul that continues to provide the glimmers that direct my path.

Green Grass And Yoga

"Do not think that love, in order to be genuine, has to be extraordinary. What we need is love without getting tired. Be faithful in small things because it is in them that your strength lies."

- Mother Teresa

Around supper time, the ambulance arrived and, still donning the semi-transparent, yellow paper gown with the thin blanket draped over me, I was helped onto a gurney. The orderlies wheeled me through the emergency room to the ambulance bay and loaded me into the back of the rig. Moments later, with sirens off, we left the VA facility and embarked on our journey to a lock-down mental health facility across town.

It took some time to navigate Friday's subsiding rush hour traffic and, when we pulled into the circle drive almost a half-an-hour later, darkness was starting to set in. Like the shadowed twilight that slowly overtakes a late afternoon sky, everything seemed murky. It was as if time had slowed down and the singular decision I had made several hours earlier was a key that was starting to unlock a reality that I was never meant to be part of.

When we finally parked in the circular driveway, the ambulance crew helped me off the gurney and into an awaiting wheelchair that would take me to the in-processing area. Fear and trepidation sat thickly in my throat as I caught a glimpse of the setting Charleston sun dipping into the Ashley River. Boats meandered lazily past the nondescript facility on their way home from a day on the salt water, skirting by the few other buildings that littered the background of the expansive grounds. There were no highwire fences or security gates. Instead, well-manicured lawns and measured foot paths bridged the gaps between the buildings, creating a serene landscape that masked the hurt and terror I felt as I was wheeled inside.

As the wheels of my mobile chair crossed the doorjamb, a flurry of activity erupted around me. Someone took my picture, capturing that moment in time, when my wrinkled, yellow paper gown, puffy, sad eyes and furrowed forehead indicated the rawness of that moment. My perceptions of control had faded, and any understanding of my future self were elusive.

Another person ushered me to a well-worn wooden chair, the scratchy upholstered seat full of stains from years of others who had, I assumed, gone through something traumatic enough to literally land them in this same seat. Once seated, someone shoved a brown clipboard and pen in my face, asking me to fill out questionnaire after questionnaire about my background, my diagnoses and my current predicament.

"*Why,*" I thought, "*can't they just call the VA and get my records sent over?*"

Within an hour, I was in the system and moved from in-processing to the substance abuse ward. I was given a pair of sweats with no drawstring, a sports bra, a t-shirt and socks to change into. Assigned to a two-bed dormitory-style room, I looked around and realized that no one had come in to clean since the last patients had been in there. The shower had matted hair circling the drain, and the toilet clearly hadn't been attended to in a while.

"This is disgusting," I said to no one in particular, as I was the only one in the room.

Sighing, I sat down on the green vinyl mattress that served as my bed.

"*Am I seriously going to have to stay here until Monday?*" I thought. "*Jesus. What did I get myself into?*"

Someone from the facility knocked briefly on the heavy wooden door, interrupting my thoughts and offering me some linens.

"Thanks," I muttered, wondering if these were the same folks who forgot to clean the drain.

Placing the fitted sheet first, and then the top sheet next, I made tiny hospital corners on each side, as I'd learned to do in boot camp. Then I covered the single vinyl pillow with a pillowcase and, once I had the bed made, I sunk down into it, letting the green vinyl mattress absorb the weight from the day as tears started to fall.

That had been the longest Friday of my life, and all of the doctors, social workers and providers who would handle my case had long since departed for the weekend. There was no one left for me to talk to. No one to walk me through next steps, to assuage my fears, or even to hold my hand, wipe the tears and, like Dr. Blackwell had earlier, let me know I would be ok.

The irony wasn't lost on me that I was in a place where safety was the biggest concern. I'd been sent there because I couldn't guarantee that I would keep myself safe. Yet, sitting on that bed, alone and terrified, I felt the most unsafe I'd ever felt in my life – which was saying a lot given my experience in African war-torn countries and in interactions on the high seas with drug runners, human traffickers, and real-life criminals. To the outsider looking in, I had been through much harder circumstances. Yet, to me, this felt like the pinnacle of them all.

This time, I had no cell phone, no books, nothing to occupy my mind. Nothing but the intrusive thoughts that kept my mind spinning with only worst-case scenarios.

"*How?*" I kept asking myself. "*How did I end up HERE? This is not for people like me. I'm supposed to be strong and competent and have my shit together.*"

Yet, there I was, and the tears that had been steadily falling since I sat down finally abated. I closed my eyes and breathed deeply, smelling only the stagnant, humid air coming from the windowless bathroom that I still didn't have enough energy or comfort to use.

I promised myself that I'd get it all sorted out in the morning and lied down, hoping for sleep. But, with the requirement to keep the bedroom door slightly open, the incessant stream of fluorescent light, originating from the bustling nurse's station, seeped into my room and infiltrated my eyelids no matter which way I positioned my head. It seemed that every time I would finally drift off into a fitful sleep, the nurse would make his or her rounds, pointing a flashlight in my face to ensure I was still alive.

At some point, a roommate showed up and settled into the unoccupied green vinyl mattress that was across the room from me. She didn't make much noise, but from the tidbits I picked up through the muffled conversation, it sounded like this wasn't her first rodeo.

As the hours passed, sunlight finally broke through the windows of the shared space right outside of my bedroom. I sat up, threw my legs over the bedframe, and stared blankly at the grey brick walls that lacked character or clarity. The room had no windows, no color, no life. It was dull. Stagnant. Stale. A symbolic reminder of what my life had become.

I went to the tiny stainless-steel sink that was affixed to the bathroom's brick wall and threw some lukewarm water on my face. Then I headed out to the common area to figure out the Plan of the Day. From my time in the Coast Guard, the Plan of the Day always offered information which provided clarity and structure and helped me understand where to be, when to be there, and what would be expected when I arrived. A small group had started to gather and were getting ready to leave the locked-down wing to head to breakfast. They would be able to go outside, transiting on one of the brick paths which led to another building where the cafeteria was housed.

"Kerver," someone said, and I looked up to find an attendant with a clipboard standing over me. "You'll need to stay here. You're not cleared yet to leave the unit."

My heart sank as I watched the assembled group leave for breakfast. The orderly promised he would bring me back some food from the cafeteria. As the last patient and he departed, I heard the click of the lock and the crushing, audible reminder that I was trapped in this nondescript brick jail, with no opportunity to leave until someone else decided when it was appropriate to give me back my freedom.

I sank into the chair next to the decrepit table that likely had seen plenty of Uno and Rummy matches over the years. Looking around the now quiet room, I heard the hushed tones of conversation from the staff who sat behind sliding glass windows, which resembled that VA waiting room I'd been in less than 24 hours prior. I couldn't discern words or distinct conversations, but all of it made me feel even more uneasy. The click, click, click of computer keystrokes filled the silent spaces and, slowly, I felt the panic creeping in. A slow burn, ascending with familiar ease, crept seditiously into my chest. The feeling of being trapped, caged, without choice, without a voice, was almost too much to bear.

"*Get it together,*" I told myself. *"You'll never get out of here if you let them see you panic.*"

I pushed the anxiety down, and, with that new Warrior Woman starting to take root, I willed the uneasiness to subside, replacing panic with logical determination. Then I made my way to the nurse's station to figure out a plan.

"When can I be discharged?" is what I started with. "I don't belong here and, since I voluntarily signed myself in, I'd like to voluntarily sign myself out."

The woman behind the glass stared at me, perplexed by my unorthodox ask. I had been compliant, so I thought my ask for an early release was reasonable.

The previous evening, I was offered a regiment of alcohol detox drugs to help me through the transition to sobriety. I declined to take the cocktail of drugs they had prescribed and, instead, agreed to drug-based therapy by acquiescing to take a small dose of Lexapro for the depression. I didn't have much hope that the Lexapro would make anything better because psychotropics never did. But I knew that I'd have to prove that I was committed to my healing journey and part of that included agreeing to take some of the suggested medications. So, despite my own fears about trying yet another psychotropic, I forced myself to comply.

"The doctors will be back on Monday," she replied. "You'll need to talk with the doctor first before a determination can be made."

That was definitely not the answer I was looking for. But I refused to be dissuaded.

"Ok," I answered, with a little more nerve. "Then I need to be moved to the regular adult unit. I shouldn't be in the substance abuse ward."

The nurse looked at me again, clearly frustrated with my persistence. Asking for my name, she flipped through my chart and made some notes. I have no idea if my agreeing to the Lexapro-based therapy factored into the final decision but, after a few moments of deliberation, she told me I would be able to transfer to the adult unit later that afternoon, once they verified a room was available.

I went back to the battered table and sat down, soaking in the silence and acknowledging my win. I could feel a warmness in my belly, an inkling of hope starting to emerge, where I began to wonder if everything would, indeed, be ok. Maybe that was my Warrior Woman starting to glow because, even in the direst of circumstances, I'd tapped into my power, used my voice, and fought for what I intuitively felt I needed.

A few hours passed before someone came to get me and transfer me over to the adult lock-down unit. Once I was settled, I went to the nurse's station to ask about next steps. The nurse who sat behind the desk, this time with no plexiglass windows, reiterated that nothing more would happen until Monday morning, when the doctor and regular staff returned to work. So much for a weekend get-away.

I left the desk and walked around the common area, noticing bookshelves lined with a variety of reading material. Finding a Bible, I went back to the nurse's station and asked if they had some paper I could use for journaling. I was issued a pencil and a small black notebook, which I took back to my room, and, like the starfish, I began to regenerate the severed areas of myself that had been damaged in this storm.

Over the remainder of the weekend, several times a day, I would escape from the noise of the common area and sit on the green vinyl mattress in my room to write. Prayer and meditation quickly became staples, helping to quiet my mind and keep me rooted and present. Journaling helped me purge all the thoughts that continued to swirl so I could stay focused on moving forward. I don't recall having any major revelations but, I can recall that my resolve and desire to fight continued to strengthen. Writing helped me regenerate my voice. I was starting, ever-so-slowly, to notice and examine the small glimmers that continued to appear as I was learning the language of my own intuition.

The weekend passed slowly, lazily, minutes crawling by on the clock. Through the windows, I watched wispy clouds perforate the blue skies as they floated past, morphing and changing on their journey. My soul was aching to get outside, to breathe air that had not been circulated through the building's filtration system, to feel the green grass in between my toes and the warmth of the October sun on my skin. I had missed the 10K race, but it didn't matter. I was exhausted, depleted, spent. So, pounding pavement for six miles may not have been the best decision for my health anyhow. Yet, my body still yearned for movement. I wanted to have the space and freedom to honor this desire, but, looking around the common area, where people sat and zoned out, there was no place that seemed suitable for even gentle movement.

When the weekend concluded, the busyness of a Monday morning settled in. My quiet time was suddenly replaced with a flurry of check ins with doctors and group therapy sessions. I was asked, several times a day, to reflect on things I could do, once I was released, to steady me. To ground me. To help me heal. My list included some of the things I was doing here, and others I knew I would start doing again once I was released. Prayer, meditation, journaling, a gratitude practice, yoga, exercise and being in nature all made it onto my list.

The need to be outside, to experience life unfiltered, intensified until I knew I had to speak up. I found a nurse.

"I was wondering," I asked her, "if there's any way we can go outside – maybe into the fenced area?"

She looked at me quizzically, clearly perplexed by my request.

"I want to be able to practice yoga in the grass," I explained. "I put on my sheet that yoga and nature are two things that help me heal."

"Um, I don't really know," she said honestly. "It's not my call – but I'll see if I can get an answer for you."

We were in a lock-down facility and, from a procedural standpoint, I guessed that there hadn't been a lot of discussion related to letting inpatients go outside.

"That would be great," I told her. "Even if it's just for a half-an-hour. I just feel like being in the sun and getting some fresh air would be really helpful."

I figured if we could be escorted to walk from one building to another for meals, why could we not be escorted to a fenced-in yard to spend some time outside? Her answer was not an immediate yes, but rather a promise that she would look into it. So, I took that as possibility and possibility means that hope may blossom.

The next day, we were granted 30 minutes in the yard for outside time, and this became a daily offering which I relished. On that first day, when the adult unit walked outside as a group, and into the fenced-in yard, I found a quiet corner where I kicked off my shoes and stood firmly rooted in the grass. I wiggled my toes and closed my eyes, breathing in the smells of grass, salt water and Charleston's crisp fall air. I listened to the birds in the nearby trees, and the boats that were transiting past on the Ashley River. My senses were once again engaging with the natural world as my body sent reminders that it needed to move. From my rooted position, where I felt grounded and safe, I started to add in small, gentle movements. I stretched out my arms into the Warrior One stance, and then created space in between my legs to allow my torso to bend over and my hands to meet the ground. I splayed my fingers wide, seeing green blades of grass emerge in between each space, and noticed the deep connection that came with having all four appendages touching the earth, together, with assured firmness. A smile slowly etched across my face and I breathed in deeply, acknowledging that moment. Even in the pain, I found my footing and began a practice of gratitude and graciousness, my emerging Warrior Woman finding peace, conviction and hope from the downward dog position.

Becoming The Badass You Were Always Meant To Be

"You don't always have to be strong. Sometimes you need to scream, swear if you have to, and have a really good cry. But you always, always need to pull yourself back together, then go back to being the badass you were meant to be."

- Author Unknown

Now with daily yoga sessions and the occasional phone call with Sarah, my mind was opening and creating space to consider what would come next. I knew that I still wasn't ready to be on my own, but the facility demanded that I have a solid plan in place before they would agree to release me. My sister offered for me to join her and her family in Austin, but my life was in Charleston. I hadn't made any decisions about continuing with the MBA coursework; however, I wanted to afford myself the opportunity to complete the course of study if I was able to figure out my mental and emotional bandwidth.

Weighing my options, I decided to ask Reilly. He had routinely visited me while I was, as I now affectionately say, *in the joint*. And, as a person who had spent time in service to others, he was familiar with trauma and understood the implications of my situation.

"So..." I started, turning to face him as he took a seat next to me in the common area, "do you think it would be ok if I stayed with you for a while?"

His hazel eyes squinted slightly, acclimating to the proximity of our positions on the couch. His ginger moustache twitched as his lips pursed gently together, his mouth working on forming an answer to my unexpected request.

"We are trying to finalize my release plans," I cut him off, interrupting any thoughts on the matter that he may have been preparing to offer. "They won't let me out of here until I have a concrete plan in place. I'm just not ready to be on my own again."

We had only known each other a couple of months and I was asking him to assume the role of part-time caretaker and step directly into the eye of my hurricane.

"Ok," he agreed without much pretense. "We can make that work."

And, just like that, with some agreed-upon ground rules in place, Reilly and I formulated a plan which would keep me safe, grounded and on my healing trajectory.

My "weekend stay" in the hospital, which had actually turned into six days, was coming to an end. Without much fanfare, the social worker pulled me aside and notified me that I was scheduled for release the following afternoon.

"Two p.m." she said, void of the excitement I felt when she uttered these words. "You'll need to make sure someone is here to pick you up."

"Yes ma'am," I nodded, recognizing that old habits die hard.

I called Reilly and let him know that he would need to be on site the following afternoon and then impatiently waited for the hours to tick by until I would see Harlie and start my next chapter. I tossed on the green vinyl mattress all night long, my skin itchy with anxiety as intrusive thoughts overtook my nervous system, offering up every possible scenario that could go wrong and prevent me from my great escape the following afternoon.

It was the same inexplicable phenomenon I'd had in boot camp, when I was nearing the eight-week mark, and inching closer to our graduation date. I hadn't done anything that would hold me back, but the anxiety of feeling like there was even an inkling of that possibility made my skin crawl.

When the sun finally rose, I was exhausted from another sleepless night. My anxiety hadn't budged and I just needed to get away from this situation. Two o'clock couldn't come fast enough. It had been a long, long time since I'd felt this way. The last time I could remember feeling this type of urgency was during my Peace Corps days when, in early 1998, a small group of my fellow Peace Corps volunteers and I were making our way from Ethiopia to Eritrea for a weekend vacation. As we sat on the poorly ventilated bus, with the windows closed tightly because a common, and widespread cultural belief led people to believe that exposure to drafts, cold air, and even moving winds – like those through bus windows – could cause sudden illness and respiratory issues, a local man asked if I wanted to exchange currency.

"I will give you 1.15 Eritrean Nakfa for each of your Ethiopian Birr," he said, in a hushed tone.

I had been warned that the authorized exchange rate was a one-to-one ratio but figured this was just a matter of convenience and the local people knew best. As a 24-year-old, it certainly didn't occur to me to wonder why he was asking me, and no one else on that crowded bus, to make a deal with him.

"Sure," I said as I reached into my pocket to pull out my Birr. And we made the exchange.

Not long after that, the bus pulled into a rural spot, parking just shy of the town's center.

"Are we stopping for lunch?" I asked another of the Peace Corps volunteers, who looked as confused as I was.

"I, I don't know," she said.

Before I could ask any more clarifying questions, a pack of machine-gun-wielding young boys entered through the bus's front door and beelined it directly to my seat. Pointing their weapons in my face, the children barked orders in a language I simply did not understand.

What I did understand was that I was in trouble.

The young boys coerced me off the bus and paraded me through the town's epicenter, with the other Peace Corps volunteers in hot pursuit. Surrounded by machine guns, I, as a "ferenji," a foreigner, was put on display for curious bystanders and townspeople.

It all felt very archaic, and terrifying.

I was led down the main street and then through a maze of twists and turns until the machine-gun-wielding boys and I finally arrived at the gated police station. As the boys pushed me through the station's front gates, my eyes fixated on rows of concrete jail cells littered throughout the compound. The whitewashed structures had no windows, and each cell had only one door. Small holes had been cut above each of these doors, which allowed air to circulate and flickers of sunlight to radiate inward. As they walked me deeper into the compound, I heard muffled, indistinguishable sounds, with the only other signs of life showing up as hands of faceless prisoners peeking through these openings.

"*Oh my God,*" I thought. "*I'm going to be locked away in this secluded prison.*"

The kids directed me over to a makeshift waiting area, with a full, bushy tree shading the small concrete slab.

"Sit," one of the kids directed, as he gestured at the concrete pad with the muzzle of his machine gun.

I looked around the small yard, only seeing hands and only hearing the moans of the incarcerated souls as they grew louder.

"*Holy shit,*" I thought as I choked down my tears. "*I'm fucked.*"

The stark realization that I had no way to contact anyone who might be able to help piqued my fight, flight or fawn response, and the logical option told me to run. But I couldn't. I was in a police compound, somewhere between Ethiopia and Eritrea, with machine guns in my personal space and a group of boys who clearly had a bone to pick with me because I had exchanged money outside of the established rates.

I inhaled sharply, the stagnant, warm air sticking to my ribs as the balsamic scent from the nearby acacia trees, and the almost peppery smell of the sun-scorched earth assaulted my olfactory senses.

Apparently, they didn't have the same one phone call rule as they did back home, so there was no way for me to reach out to Peace Corps leadership, or the U.S. Embassy, to ask for help. I was trapped, left wondering if I was going to rot in this suffocating compound.

"How long do you think we will be?" I asked the guard who had replaced the young kids and seemed quite disinterested in his temporary assignment.

"Until they get back," he answered.

"Until who gets back?" I pushed.

It was clear that the guard wasn't interested in answering any more questions, so I was left mulling this unanswered question while I wondered whether I would ever be released.

Without any other alternatives, I waited in the brutal heat until the police chief, and his entourage, returned from their hours-long meeting.

"Ah," the police chief said with a hint of arrogance when he finally arrived and was briefed on the situation. "I understand you exchanged money on the bus." He was staring at me. "One Birr for 1.15 Nafka. Hmm?" The last part of his statement, sounding more accusatory than contemplative.

"Yes." I nodded, acknowledging my predicament but trying to remain grounded. Compliant.

"That is unfortunate," he said as he leisurely scanned the compound and then turned his head squarely towards me, fixing his eyes on my own. "Very unfortunate."

I breathed again, deeply, fully, expanding my diaphragm and rib cage until there was zero negative space to be had. I had spent years refining these techniques, often turning to my breath as a soothing balm in times of stress or crisis, when I knew I could apply it, like a salve, to calm my vagus nerve.

He looked at me as he made his final decision. "You should go," he stated matter-of-factly and waved absently in my direction.

"Go?" I asked.

"Go," he replied. And then he stood up and walked away.

With permission granted to leave without any further consequences, my legs took over before my head caught up, and I sprinted out of the police compound to the first bus I saw, hoping to get as far away from this town, and situation, as possible.

"Sue," the social worker said, arousing me from my daydream. "These are the guidelines you'll need to follow once you leave."

I glanced at her thick fingers, grasping a clipboard in one hand and a stack of discharge papers in the other. It was almost time.

"Take a look through them and let me know if you have questions. Once you have completed that, we can get you over to billing to complete the out-processing paperwork, and then you'll be free to go."

Go. There was that word again. The one that explicitly implied freedom, yet remained ambiguous in defining a particular direction, path, or destination.

After that harrowing week, the transition back to even a baseline of normality was excruciating. Every day was an opportunity to improve – even if it was just by one percent. But, those percentages, over time, added up and became cumulative. As the weeks turned into months, I allowed myself to excavate and examine deeper crevices of my life with a critically honest lens. Under the microscope, it became painfully obvious that I had not been living the healthy lifestyle I believed I had been. I was a train wreck, and I couldn't hide from that fact any longer.

When I contemplated the disconnect, I understood that, for decades, it had been easier to placate negative emotions and circumstances with bourbon and beer, Cabernet and cocktails than it was to face dark and scary circumstances head-on, deconstructing them until I was able to uncover and deal with their root causes. Now, though, I was in an entirely different playing field. Different rules. Different approaches. Different outcomes.

After being discharged, I started to test the waters of sobriety and sought out safe and supportive ways where I would be surrounded by women with similar experiences. I went back to the VA, seeking comprehensive outpatient therapy to build on the momentum I had gained during my week of inpatient treatment. I asked to be placed in veteran-based women's groups because I wanted to share my story and my fears about the journey that lay ahead. What I found was that these resources did not exist. What did exist was co-ed weekly group therapy that I was thrust into, complete with older men, many of whom donned service-specific ballcaps and talked of days gone by instead of their emotions, their trauma, their hope and their healing.

"*There's no way,*" I said to myself after sitting through the first group session. Of the 15 seats around the conference room table, three of us were women, and there was little space and opportunity afforded to us, or our voices, during the hour-long session. They told me to trust the process, but this was one process that seemed completely broken.

I was tired of feeling unseen and unheard and I was so tired of having to constantly battle for the care, and the connection, I knew my healing required.

"*Why is this so difficult?*" I asked myself.

I just couldn't crack the code. Things that should have been simple, like getting an appointment to see a mental health provider, seemed even harder than finding a women veteran's group. I was told it would be months until I could get an appointment which, logically, seemed unreasonable for someone who was recently released from inpatient care. I needed medication monitoring and weekly one-on-one counseling sessions. I needed people who would listen, understand, and empathize without judgment or blame. I needed a community.

I spent weeks after my discharge doing research, making phone calls and finding people to ask for what I knew I needed. I began by calling the Women's Advocate at the VA, which did not produce any results. Next, I called the VA Patient Advocate, which also resulted in zero solutions. It didn't take me much time to understand that I was all I had and that I would have to advocate for myself. I had to be relentless, assertive and clear about what I needed. It was like being in the Service all over again, and that incongruency I had once felt between needing to be aggressive and wanting to be compassionate was resurfacing. But this time I knew I had a choice and could embrace both parts and pieces of myself with care and confidence.

"*You've done hard things,*" I told myself. "*You can do this.*" I repeated that simple mantra many, many times each day until they became words I would live by. A simple reminder that I was cloaked in strength and dignity and held the power to turn self-doubt into self-trust.

So, despite the barriers, the setbacks, and the number of times the word *no* outnumbered a *yes*, I pushed. And then I pushed harder until, after multiple weeks of *no's* and *I don't knows*, and feeling like I was getting nowhere, I'd had enough.

I called the White House and launched a Congressional complaint against Charleston's VA hospital.

Within a few days, I received a call from the head of the hospital's mental health department, assuring me I would be able to be seen immediately. The wheels were finally moving and, before I knew it, I was enrolled into weekly one-on-one counseling sessions with, in a full-circle moment, Dr. Blackwell.

A Beach Cruiser And A Meatball

"If you don't like something, change it. If you can't change it, change your attitude."
– Maya Angelou

Dr. Blackwell and I had been meeting for a few weeks when one morning, after one of our sessions, I felt the intuitive glimmer to stop by the VA Director's office. I'd learned to start paying attention to these feelings and, instead of dismissing the invitation as something that seemed silly, I took a right out of Dr. Blackwell's office, bypassed the elevators, and followed the maze of corridors until I reached the executive suite of offices.

As I entered through the glass door of the executive suite, I found myself standing in an expansive waiting area with very few chairs. Directly across the room was a titanic oak desk, purposefully positioned to the left of the corridor connecting the waiting area to the suite of executive offices. A woman rested behind the desk, only bothering to glance up from her computer because I had the audacity to close the gap between us.

"Good morning," I said, as I approached her perch.

I couldn't tell if she was the gatekeeper for all of the executives or just for the head honcho. So, I proceeded with caution.

"I'm wondering if I might be able to speak with the director." It was a simple question, posed as a statement, but as unlikely as finding a screen door on a submarine.

She stopped typing for the briefest of moments.

“Do you have an appointment?” she queried.

“I don’t,” I countered. “But I do have some concerns.”

I was on a mission to share my experience with getting mental health appointments and follow-on care, including all the unnecessary delays and hoops I had to endure to get the attention I needed. But this wasn’t about complaining. Instead, my goal was to share lessons learned and offer suggestions so the hospital could improve their processes and women veterans could forgo jumping through the same hoops.

She looked back at her computer, scrolling through calendars to see if she could get me scheduled with someone.

“You can make an appointment,” she offered. “What is this about?”

"I’ve had to advocate for myself to figure out how to get care here," I said. "My concern is that many of my veteran sisters are in the same position. Fed up. Exhausted. And when people get exhausted, they quit.” I emphasized that last word.

I held her stare, as she locked in.

“Quitting shouldn't be an option. But, when women are put into positions where we have to keep asking, to keep pushing, to keep fighting when the only answers we ever get are ‘I don’t know’ or ‘our programs aren’t designed to address that,’ the whole process seems futile. The problem is…”

I paused briefly to gather my thoughts.

“The problem is that it's hard to reach out for help in the first place. So, when women hear ‘no’ so many times, they stop trying to get to ‘yes.’ We are caretakers, nurturers, moms, and all things to all people. Our families, our spouses, our jobs rely on us for support, for guidance, for survival. We give all we have to keep things going and, if we have anything left over to put towards our own self-care, we are left trying to navigate a system that was never designed for us."

I glanced down, noticing my hands were now clenched in fists that were tightly pulled next to the inseams of my jeans. I was standing at "Attention," a position signifying honor and respect. As I stood rooted in my anger, hurt and rage, I only felt dishonored and disrespected, a direct result of my lived experience. And I'd had enough.

This was about so much more than healthcare. It was about reclaiming the power that an entire system had tried to erase. It was about speaking up, and speaking out, creating agency for women's contributions, intelligence, compassion, bravery and integrity that became the glue which held everything, and everyone, together. The healthcare system was indicative of a larger construct that was inadequate, inequitable, and protected the deeply buried, dark secret that women were needed, but they certainly weren't valued. And my Warrior Woman was pissed.

I released my fingers from my tightened grip. "Women veteran suicide rates are increasing because we are tired. We are tired of asking for help we can't get. We are tired of trying to fit into a structure that was never built to handle our uniqueness. And we are tired of convincing ourselves, and others, that anyone cares."

I inhaled sharply.

"Things have to change," I said. "So, I am making it my mission to advocate for those who can't or won't advocate for themselves. And," I added, "for every single woman who no longer has the strength to do it herself."

She stopped looking for a date on the calendar and stood up. Gently placing her hands on my shoulders, she directed me back across the executive suite and towards the elevators.

"I want to show you something," she said.

We arrived on the first floor, the elevator doors opening to reveal a set of large glass doors with the VA logo etched across the pair. As we pulled the doors open, noise, busyness and activity created a scene that was chaotic yet magnificently controlled. The front desk team member attended to ringing phones while a handful of other employees handled endless requests for clothing, bus passes and other sundry items from a smattering of veterans who had critical needs.

The scene was overwhelming.

As my eyes scanned the bedlam, I noticed three office spaces on the left side of the room, and three on the right. Each office had a door, which, with all the activity, offered little in the way of privacy. There was a large wall, about three quarters of the way back from where we stood, that had cabinet space on the adjacent side and doubled to hide several desks, computers, and phones.

"This is our Voluntary Services department," the woman said as we continued our impromptu visit. "Voluntary Services oversees all the volunteers and donations for this hospital and our affiliated clinics."

Piles of donated clothes, non-perishable food items and other items cluttered the space. My eyes darted from one pile of donations to another, watching the orchestrated giving.

"*I wonder if they had a sports bra I could have worn under my yellow paper gown.*" The irony of this moment wasn't lost on me.

We took a few more steps into the lion's den, when one of the employees approached us with her warm smile.

"Sue is interested in signing up as a volunteer," the administrative assistant said before I could comprehend what was happening.

"Wait. What?" I spun around, giving her a puzzled look, amazed at how quickly my declaration to advocate for other female veterans had morphed into a veiled commitment to sign up as a volunteer. This was never part of the plan.

I was still enrolled in my MBA program, and I didn't know how volunteering would factor into the time I had to focus on my coursework. I'd missed an entire week of the program as a result of my hospitalization, and end-of-course exams were right around the corner. The required European trip was coming up quickly, and, given all that had happened, I knew there was no way I'd be able to go on a trip across the pond. Nevertheless, I wanted to make sure there was a way for me to complete all of the remaining requirements and get credit for the work I had done.

I thanked everyone for their time and left the hospital with more questions than I'd had when I entered that day. Did I want to volunteer? Was that the best way to advocate for and help my sisters? And what about this MBA situation?

I glanced at my phone and noticed that it was closing in on the time I had scheduled to speak with College of Charleson's leadership team to try and work through next steps.

"Hello Sue," the principal member said, as I picked up the phone at that appointed time. His resolute voice reverberated through my headset. "I'm calling to find out what's happening. And how you are." The last part of his statement came out almost as an afterthought.

"I'm ok," I said, matching his neutrality with my own. "I guess you know I missed class due to some unforeseen circumstances."

That was as much on that topic as I was willing to offer. "I just need to know how I can complete my finals, and this semester, because I won't be able to come back to campus, and I can't make the class trip."

I might as well have said I was dropping out of the MBA program, as it had been made clear from the first day of class that the trip to Europe was non-negotiable for graduation.

The line was silent for a beat. "I'm sorry to hear that. But, the program requirements specify that the class trip is a requirement for graduation. If you can't make it to campus to complete your finals, or to Europe, you won't be able to complete the MBA program."

"Huh," I said dryly. I could feel my rough, sharp edges taking over. So much for neutrality. Surely it couldn't be as black-and-white as that. I had spent an entire Coast Guard career learning how to adapt to dynamic and unexpected situations and always found creative solutions to insurmountable problems. I'd been able to get fuel for our vessel when the delivery routes in the country we were visiting for a port call were shutting down due to civil unrest. I'd figured out how to get parts for our reverse osmosis drinking water system air dropped by a C-130 when we were 200 nautical miles offshore. And I'd stood on a flight deck for over an hour, in the brutal heat of an unrelenting equatorial sun, speaking with foreign customs agents over the satellite phone, to obtain clearance for a helicopter rotor blade to be delivered to the port where we would be mooring in less than 48 hours.

I'd navigated complexity, uncertainty and ambiguity, always finding a solution to insurmountable problems. I was tenacious and stubborn, and I certainly wasn't ready to let one man determine my future, without at least having a more informed conversation.

"There's got to be another option," I offered to this man who did not seem amenable to embracing the gray.

"Again, the requirements for graduation are what they are," he said. "There's not much I can do."

When we hung up, I opened my computer to see what else *I* could do. A quick Google search revealed that the college offered certain accommodations through their Center for Disability Services and, with a bit more research, a few completed forms, and a handful of email exchanges with my professors, I constructed a plan that would allow me to finish my remaining coursework at home and take my final exams in an alternate location so I didn't have to return to the classroom. The question about the European trip remained unresolved and, after an in-person meeting with the college's leadership, it was brutally evident that, while I would get full credit for the semester's work, there was no way to complete the program unless I went abroad. So, at the end of what had been a very long semester, I decided it was time to sever this relationship. I applied to The Citadel and, upon acceptance, transferred my credits to their more traditional MBA program and completed my degree a year-and-a-half later.

But I still hadn't decided about how I wanted to serve female veterans, or about volunteering at the VA.

Winter and spring crept by, and by the time boating season was in full swing, I finally felt strong enough to move out of Reilly's house and transition back to my little garage apartment. Many of my friends remained unaware of my weeklong stint in the hospital and I didn't yet have the courage to tell them the story. But I did tell them that I had decided to stop drinking and, with an air of decisiveness and finality, left it at that. Most were receptive when they realized this was a non-negotiable and ceased to question my choice. But, to ease the burden of any unwanted interrogation, I arrived at Low Country crawfish boils and backyard barbecues with my constant plus one - a Yeti tumbler containing iced-down non-alcoholic wine, or a mix of cranberry and seltzer water. Boat and beach trips became infinitely easier when I remembered to bring my own cooler so I could refill that Yeti tumbler at my leisure.

I eventually eased into a life that was void of hangovers and headaches and, with things appearing manageable for the first time in many, many moons, I relaxed enough to settle into a healing rhythm and welcome small moments of joy throughout each day. I savored the simplicity of smelling the sweet magnolia blooms in my backyard and took long bike rides through Mount Pleasant and Sullivans Island with Harlie, who accompanied me in her orange doggie trailer that was affixed to the back of my yellow and blue beach cruiser.

One afternoon, as Harlie and I cruised down one of the sidewalks on the way to the beach, I noticed a southern cottage with a “For Sale” sign in the lawn. I hadn’t really given much consideration to purchasing my own place, but, on this bright summer day, the idyllic house beckoned and the idea took shape. I knew I was ready to dip my toes back into the work world, which meant I would have the financial resources to purchase a bungalow. So, I contacted a realtor, who obliged me with a showing. It turned out that this southern cottage was not the one, but the seed had been planted. We continued the search, and, after several showings, I stumbled upon a three-bedroom ranch house that was four miles from the beach. Despite the popcorn ceilings and laminate floors, I intuitively knew that this was the place where I could grow and thrive. So, I put an offer in, and, after the requisite back-and-forth, finally got the acceptance phone call as I was on my way into the gym for a late day workout.

By the end of June, I'd moved in. The popcorn ceilings had been scraped, the laminate floors had been replaced with barnwood-style vinyl planks, and the simple cottage, which, ironically, sat just around the corner from the 600-square-foot apartment where I almost ended it all, became my cozy, safe nest where I could retreat, relax and continue to recover.

On the first of September, after being in my new home for a few months, I found myself in crisis yet again. Harlie and I had gone to Folly Beach on a bluebird sky Saturday morning so she could play in the waves and scamper through the sand. We spent most of the day outside, which should have given her a voracious appetite. So, when she didn't eat her dinner, I knew I had to take her to the emergency vet. Reilly was out of town, and I couldn't manage to get Harlie's 80 pounds of floof into my 4Runner by myself. I called the local police department, and they sent an officer to help. Within a few minutes of his arrival, he had Harlie packed into a towel like a taco, loaded into my truck, and we were on the way to the emergency vet.

Once there, Harlie and I were set up in a sterile exam room, and the vet came in expeditiously.

"Sue," her soothing voice cut through the stale room as her hands examined Harlie's legs, head and throat. "Tell me what's going on."

"I'm not sure," I responded matter-of-factly. "We went to Folly Beach this morning and everything was fine. Then we got home and tonight, she wouldn't eat. She always eats…"

My voice trailed off and I watched the vet continue her exam. She was methodical and calculated, with an exactness that indicated that she was looking for something specific.

"Well," the doctor looked up from Harlie's brown fur, her left hand resting on Harlie's extended abdomen, "it would be best if we run some tests."

"Ok."

The lab tech came in the room with a stainless-steel gurney and, with help from another colleague, the two hoisted Harlie on the metal frame and prepared to wheel her away. It was a scene that felt a little too familiar.

"I love you Little Bits," I told her, placing a mommy kiss on her nose and rubbing that soft space in between her ears. "I love you so, so much."

They wheeled her into the back room and invited me to make myself comfortable in the chair of the sterile exam room. It smelled of musty fur and bleach, and I wondered how many dog moms had sat in this chair and cried for their fur baby.

I looked at my phone, and decided I needed to call J.P. We hadn't really talked since our divorce, but Harlie had been our dog, and I knew I owed him the courtesy of a phone call.

"Hey," I said dryly when he picked up.

"Hey," he responded with the same monosyllabic tone I had offered. "What's up?"

"It's Harlie," my voice cracked, and he knew the situation wasn't good.

Even after all we had been through, and a divorce that absolutely crushed me, J.P. showed up in that moment with compassion and grace. And that's when I knew we would slowly, over time, be able to mend what had been severed and reestablish our relationship simply as friends.

"Oh. Is she ok?"

"I…I don't know." Tears streamed down my face, hitting the speckled laminate floor that was littered with remnants of her fur pooled in tiny, random clumps. "They've taken her in the back for some tests. I have no idea. I just don't know what to do."

"Well, you can start by breathing," he offered, reminding me that I needed air in my lungs if I was going to stay steady and alert.

I breathed in sharply.

"*One. Two. Three. Four.*" I exhaled slowly, silently counting my breaths and allowing my nervous system to untwist, just a little bit, as I teed myself up for another inhale. "*One. Two. Three. Four.*" I silently counted again, filling my lungs with life-giving oxygen as J.P. waited patiently on the other end of the line.

I continued for a few more cycles and then finally broke the silence. "I just don't want to lose her. She's been my ride-or-die, and I don't know what I would do without her."

"I get it," J.P. offered. Years earlier, we collectively made the choice to adopt Harlie from a man who no longer had a use for her. As a puppy, Harlie had been trained to hunt birds. But, at some point, she lost interest in the game and, to that man, became what he would call a failed hunting dog. But, to us, she was perfect.

Harlie was wild when we first got her, eating television remote controls and slippers and trying to figure out her place in our little family. But, over time, as we showered her with love, routine and the reassurance that we would take care of her, no matter what, Harlie became an incredible companion. She was pure love, all heart, fiercely independent, but loyal to a T. She was a Warrior, a fighter, and the keeper of my heart.

"I don't know what to tell you, Sue," J.P. breathed into the phone. "Maybe see what the tests say and then let me know."

I agreed to keep him apprised and had just hung up the phone when the vet came back in.

Her look told me everything I needed to know. Harlie was gone. She had crossed over to the Rainbow Bridge on her own accord, deciding she was done living with the cancer that I didn't even know she had been battling.

I sat in the quiet of that sterile exam room, processing the events of the evening.

"*Why?*" I wondered, "*Why does everything I love leave me so unexpectedly? Why is everything so fucking hard?*" And then my heart shattered again.

Harlie had been my buddy, my constant companion, the one who forced me out of the house and back into nature so I could start to heal. I drove home alone, sensing the distinct emptiness in the back of the 4Runner, where Harlie should have been. When I finally reached my bedroom, I burrowed deep under the safety of the heavy blankets that sat atop the queen-sized bed and wept until I had no tears left. Then I fell into an exhausted, fitful slumber.

I spent the next two days in that bed, doomscrolling through social media feeds and searching for anything that would distract me from the incessant ache of my broken heart. Then it happened. I stumbled upon a video feed of "Lucy and the Chocolate Factory" - a litter of chocolate lab puppies which would soon be up for adoption from an animal rescue facility near Atlanta. As I watched their puppy shenanigans through my iPhone screen, the fog lifted. I watched them learn to eat kibble, learn to play outside in the sun, learn to trust their human caretakers and learn to ask for what they wanted through side-eye glances and whiny, guttural sounds. I couldn't get enough of these little nuggets, and my heart was opening to possibility.

It had only been a few weeks since Harlie's passing when the shelter held an online fundraising event. People could suggest names for these littles, and the highest bidders got to name the pack. As I swiped, searching for the final names, I came upon a snapshot of a perfectly round, brown chocolate hound with a smudge of red nail polish on his behind. Up until this point, the nail polish color was used as his identification marker. But now, this guy had a name. The fundraiser winner had coined him "Meatball," and my heart melted. I kept my eye on him, watching him through the pixels on my screen. He was a messy eater, a disaster around the water bowl, and the friendliest, goofiest, most lovable chunk of chocolate lab love I'd ever seen.

I knew we were meant to be best buds.

So, on October 21, 2018, just one week shy of the 365-day mark since my yellow paper gown escapade, I drove down to Georgia and brought Meatball home.

Long Walks And Big Talks

"Love and compassion are necessities, not luxuries. Without them, humanity cannot survive."

- Dalai Lama

Six days after Meatball's homecoming, I penned these words on Facebook:

Today marks one year of sobriety. One year ago was one of the darkest days of my life. I was trying to put the pieces of a shattered life back together, while refusing to deal with the reasons why it was so shattered in the first place.

It was time for a change, and I had to face my demons head-on and advocate for my life. I had to start to believe I was worth fighting for and give into the realization that I couldn't do it on my own. So, I sought help and I prayed.

I prayed for grace and forgiveness. I prayed that I could accept where I was and let go of the past. I prayed I would find ways to be a light to myself and others. And I prayed for the strength and the patience to walk the walk as I grew to love myself and fight for the things worthwhile. We all are worth fighting for – every life, every breath, every dream, every moment.

Sharing openly for the first time was a powerful experience that led me to consider how I could continue to build a healthy, whole, and thriving lifestyle. Unfortunately, a continued relationship with Reilly didn't factor into that equation.

By the end of 2018, as I continued to put the pieces of my life back together, I was offered a paid position as the Voluntary Services Manager at the same VA hospital where I'd been admitted the prior year. I was now supervising the same group of people who had compassionately greeted me when I showed up with the administrative assistant and been asked to volunteer. On that visit, the idea that I would be overseeing this program, this group of professionals, never crossed my mind. And, while I can honestly say I never saw it coming, I can't say I was entirely surprised when it arrived. People often capitulate to the idea that hindsight is 20/20. I would agree and I would add that our paths in life are not always linear but, when we retrospectively look back and see how the pieces connect, often, it all makes sense.

Coming to the Charleston VA Hospital as an employee, instead of a patient, provided a daily reminder of how far I had progressed along my healing journey. My Warrior Woman continued to protect my sobriety with fierce doggedness, with the commitment to self that when and if the Alcohol Siren beckoned, I wouldn't – couldn't – heed that call. I came from a long family history of alcoholism, from parents who both suffered from addiction, and other family members who followed their lead. The overindulgence created unnecessary turmoil in my formative years and in my adult life. History had proven that one drink always became two. Two always became three. Three turned into Sloppy Sue and, before I knew it, I was on the road to blackout drunk. Imbibing was a slippery slope that I no longer was willing to slide down because, that "just one drink" had almost cost me everything.

As I settled into the rhythms of a regular schedule, and Meatball and I nested in our new home, I leaned into doing the things that created peace, including yoga, writing, long walks and fly fishing. In April of 2019, I was invited to go on my first fly fishing retreat with *Project Healing Waters*, a veteran fly fishing organization on a mission to foster resilience, connections and community. The invitation was to travel to Montana with seven other veterans, and fish on the Bighorn River, which is a world-renowned blue-ribbon trout fishery. I accepted that invitation and spent a week finding joy and laughter on the river.

A few months later, in October, the day before my second soberversary, I finally completed the James Island Connector 10K. My Warrior Woman was testing the waters, and shortly after the race, in this pivotal public admission on Facebook, I experienced another ah-ha moment. I decided to play big, to step out from my shadow and allow myself to try on the cape of transparency. I wasn't sure what to expect, especially because this was the first public admission of my hospital stay and I was now working at the hospital where it had all begun. So, I made a very intentional choice and penned the following:

Every day we lose 22 veterans to suicide. And every day I realize I was so close to being another statistic.

Today I finished the James Island Connector 10K — which was something I signed up to do two years ago but missed because I was in the hospital. I decided I no longer wanted to live.

My life had completely fallen apart and I was broken to the core. I was so, so lost and was filling the void with wine, whiskey, beer and any other alcoholic concoction that would numb the pain.

Tomorrow marks 2 years of sobriety. Everyone thinks sobriety is hard — but I've found it so liberating. Instead of drinking, I have filled my life with things that fill my soul. And I've been surrounded by a Village who has supported me and helped me move past fear, crippling doubt and negative self-talk.

Today symbolized all the things that are RIGHT in my life. We all have purpose. We all have talent. And we all have worth. Please continue to be that love and light — because you never know when your words and actions can positively change a life.

After hitting post, I steeled myself for the backlash, judgement, sarcasm and maybe even pity that I was sure would populate the comment section. I was looking for connection, and wasn't sure what I would do if negativity seeped in. But it was worth the risk, because I no longer wanted to sit on the sidelines and hope that things would change. I wanted to be a woman of action, and I wanted to stay true to my word. I had made a promise, to myself, and to other women, that I would advocate for those who felt like they didn't have a voice. So, I needed to see what it would look and feel like to use mine unabashedly.

What I wasn't prepared for was the overwhelming feedback that offered support, encouragement, commiseration and peace. I had shared a peek at my underbelly, the icky, sticky parts that I wanted to keep hidden, and people connected. Some even shared parts of their stories and that connective tissue let me see the power of voice, and how words could be used to heal, instead of hurt.

It had only been two years since I'd felt abandoned, forgotten and unloved. But the tides were starting to turn, and I was trusting and taking action on the Divine glimmers, which appeared in all sorts of ways. Sometimes they would show up as gut feelings.

Other times it was in repetitive signs. And, then, there was the occasional email, like the one I'd received about Odin.

The animal shelter, where I'd adopted Meatball, sent me a note to let me know that they had just received a senior Golden Retriever which had been abandoned in an Atlanta suburb. The family he'd known all his life had left him on the streets, to fend for himself, when they moved away. With so much trust and love that dogs naturally offer their human families, I was heartbroken by this news. Odin's situation felt symbolic and eerily familiar, as I knew the searing pain of having love unceremoniously stripped away, and being left to figure out how to navigate an entirely new state of existence. I knew I couldn't let Odin go through the same fate, so I chose to take him in, give him my heart, and provide a safe home and all the support he needed to have the best twilight tour imaginable. I headed to Atlanta and picked up my second fur baby, whom I'd have for only 16 more months before he too crossed the Rainbow Bridge.

As we were adjusting to our family of three, COVID-19 started making its way from international headlines to the local news. And, working at a hospital, I knew things were about to amp up. One morning, as I sat in my cubicle, pecking away at my computer keyboard, a middle-aged, dark-haired woman, floated through the office's glass doors. Her mega-watt smile lit up the room, and everyone greeted her with hugs and smiles. Her essence created the feeling of being with an old friend, that one trusted soul who cradles your heart and covers your spirit like a warm blanket. Her enthusiastic hugs gave my heart as much of a boost as the double-shot vanilla latte I had been nursing, and I was glad to be able to take a break from my computer screen to engage with this beautiful woman.

"Hey Karen!" I called when she finally made it within ear shot of my office. "How are things?"

"Hi Sue!" she responded with enthusiasm, despite the threat of a worldwide pandemic that was knocking at our door.

Karen was a program manager with the American Red Cross and always had creative, well-positioned ideas to meet the varying needs of our complex veteran community.

"It sounds like things are going to get crazy," she said, referencing the chaos that was emerging on social media and in the news.

"No doubt," I responded. "I'm just working on some contingency plans, trying to figure out options in case things get really bad."

I stared at my screen, trying to predict what might be on the horizon, and the best way to plan for a worst-case scenario. I remembered my Coast Guard days, working through natural disasters and managing a myriad of crises. I thought I was done with the complexities of crisis response, yet here I sat, working through the crisis management playbook, as if this was a routine and predictable part of my job.

I sighed heavily.

"We should walk," Karen offered.

"Like – right now?" I was obviously confused because my workday was just beginning and I was not dressed for a romp at the beach.

"No. I mean, after work. Or on a Saturday. Let's go for a walk and relieve some of this stress."

It would have been so easy to say no, and find an excuse to brush off the invitation. As a middle-aged woman, engaging with new people was hard. But something deep inside of me urged me to lean in, and invited me to listen to this Divine glimmer.

"Ok," I agreed. "How about Saturday?"

We agreed on a meeting time and location and, after a hectic work week, took to the streets of Mount Pleasant. As we put some miles under our feet, Karen and I talked about COVID, work, her kids, and our shared military service experiences as female veterans.

I felt an immediate connection and my walls began to crumble. Trust was a difficult concept for me. I had a hard time trusting things would work out, and an even harder time putting faith and confidence in people, because people usually were the source of trauma, heartache, disappointment and hurt.

Yet, Karen made trusting easy.

I often wondered, "*how does an adult actually make friends?*" I suppose book clubs, online event-based groups and Bible studies are a great place to start; but I found that I wanted to be able to build the trust I needed to share my heart. I craved the type of friendships that afforded me space to show up without pretense or the obligation to appear put-together if I felt messy and unhinged.

Karen was this kind of person for me.

As COVID-19 crept into our South Carolina bubble, Karen rallied her Red Cross volunteers and, before I could truly process the gravity of the entire situation, bags of cloth masks came pouring through our double doors. Concurrently, my team was pivoting, seeking creative ways to keep our volunteers occupied, while figuring out how to meet the increasingly complex needs of the veteran patients in a world that was diminishing and closing us all in.

That's when Karen approached me with an idea.

"Sue," she said one morning as she stood in the makeshift door of my tiny cubicle office, "you know how the Red Cross has been offering resiliency workshops for Military Sexual Trauma (MST) survivors?"

She looked at me for acknowledgement, but I had none to offer.

"Um, no, I actually didn't know that was a thing," I replied.

"Yeah, well," she continued, "these workshops have been a safe space – especially for female veterans – to share their experiences and support one another while doing art therapy. But they've been in person, and, with COVID, we obviously can't do that now."

"Uuuugh." I groaned. "This stupid virus is messing everything up!"

"What if it doesn't?" Karen asked.

"What do you mean?"

"What if we figure out a way to do these workshops online?"

My immediate thought went to the logistical concerns of doing a resiliency workshop through Zoom.

"How would that even work?" I countered, running through a list of possible craft items that each veteran would need for the art therapy portion. "I mean, how are you going to get sticky googly eyes, paint, birdhouses, or whatever you use for the art projects to each participant, in time for their workshop? And what about HIPPA compliance?"

"Sue," Karen said, rolling her own metaphorical googly eyes at me, "it doesn't have to be that complicated."

"Ok then. Walk me through it."

We spent the next half hour hashing out the particulars of not only getting art therapy supplies to the veterans but also ensuring we could document any positive outcomes that resulted from this idea while maintaining HIPPA standards. As Karen described her plan, my creative juices started to flow.

"If we are using an online platform," I asked, "do we have to limit participation just to our local veterans?"

"Maybe not!" Karen's eyes lit up. "We can assemble the art kits here," she suggested, pointing to some space on one of the tables in the common area, "and then mail them to the participants. And, if we do it that way, we can open participation to more MST survivors who are feeling isolated and alone."

"Yes!" I exclaimed, wrapping my head around the possibility of offering encouragement, creativity and community to these veterans in a time when safety and security were rapidly vanishing commodities.

As Karen and I flushed out the details, I recognized how harrowing MST could be for the survivors. In my own story, I had plenty of examples of gender disparity, overt discrimination, and a few disturbing close calls from years gone by. But I was never physically assaulted. So, I never believed that MST was an applicable term for what I had experienced. And, it wouldn't be until the next year, when I was receiving treatment for major depression, that memories would surface which provided a very persuasive counterargument to this flawed logic.

The resiliency workshops were a success, and, a few years later, on the podcast, Karen and I talked about the impacts that resulted from that office conversation.

"We had maybe 20 to 25, depending on the group," she shared. "We built bird houses during MST Awareness Month. We made baskets out of wooden blocks. We did face masks during PTSD Awareness Month, and we crocheted, we painted, we built moccasins, we sewed purses. Any kind of art that was suggested, we did."

"Did you have a lot of men who were participating in the MST activities?" I asked her.

"I was under the impression that it was limited to females at the time when we first started these groups," Karen admitted. "And, during some of the discussions during our PTSD groups, I learned that men had it. We had a lot more men, believe it or not, who wanted to do art than ladies."

The fact that MST was gender-neutral never occurred to me. Which, retrospectively, was a closed-minded and absolutely ridiculous thing to think. People are people, and the military is a broad array of humans, who come from all walks of life, belief systems and backgrounds. So, it would make sense that harmful actions could happen to anyone, regardless of their pronouns.

"We've kept the group separate," Karen said. "Obviously, men and women need that little bit of distance so they can feel free, they can share with each other, peer to peer. We do have some groups that are co-ed, but not too many."

"Have some of these people who had only met virtually now had the chance to meet in person?" I asked her, recognizing that, at this time, we were four years post COVID.

"Some of our groups are back in person. A lot of the groups, especially the MST group for the females, are still virtual because those ladies are all over the country. It's not just here in South Carolina. We are allowing them to join us from different locations."

"So, this local program ended up going national?" I asked.

"It did," Karen noted. "It was a program that I started in the Charleston, Buford, Myrtle Beach areas. We expanded it through our state. It went into our whole division, which makes up 10 states, and then it went national."

I was awestruck.

"It's funny how it all started," Karen confirmed. "I had just started with the Red Cross, and I was determined that I was going to come back to South Carolina, and I was going to own something. I kept getting shot down, shot down, shot down. And then finally, I said, you know what, can I just come in and do art? And that's where it took off. That's when I met you. And we brought in resiliency, we brought in art to the VA, and it has been a very strong, supported program ever since."

I was flabbergasted as I realized that the glimmers I'd followed in supporting Karen's idea were about so much more than assembling art kits. The glimmers were about starting a movement that would allow MST survivors to find solace, connection, community and voice, regardless of where they lived.

one shot. It went into a whole division, which turned into [illegible] states, and then it went nationally."

I was astounded.

"It's funny how things started," Karen continued. "I had just started with the Pell Grant and I was determined that I was going to come back to school and I was going to do something, instead of getting put down and down and down and down. Then finally I said, you know what, I'm finally going to dream, and [illegible] that's when I met you. So we brought in resiliency, we brought [illegible] to the [illegible], it has become very strong, supported program ever since."

I was flabbergasted. I realized that the [illegible] [illegible] supporting someone [illegible] under [illegible] attacks. [illegible] was about starting a movement that would allow [illegible] community [illegible] of where they lived.

Rugged Spaces, Wild Places

"What if...everything you are going through right now is preparing you for a dream bigger than you can imagine?"
- Author Unknown

As COVID progressed, fly fishing shifted from an occasional recreational sport to a critical part of my healing journey. I'd tapped into the essence of it during the *Project Healing Waters* trip to Montana, and, again, when I went on an all-women's fly fishing trip to Alaska. Connecting with a group of seven other ladies helped me find parts of myself that had been dormant for decades. I got to build those relationships just before social distancing, masks and hand sanitizer complicated the in-person opportunities. Pre-COVID, I left for the remoteness of King Salmon, Alaska, uncertain if my rudimentary fly fishing abilities would be adequate enough for this type of trip. I was terrified to put myself in such a vulnerable position because I knew I would be relying heavily on the guides, and likely some of the other ladies, to carry me through. But, as I would see time and time again, there was power in women joining together, and in Alaska's wildest places, community and connection was born.

We caught an awful lot of fish. We saw an awful lot of wildlife. And we had an awful lot of fun. My experience in Alaska amplified my appreciation, not only for fly fishing, but for wildlife and fisheries conservation, which would serve me well in later years.

As I thought back to my arrival at King Salmon's regional airport, which was a remote location almost 300 miles southwest of Anchorage, I felt empowered and emboldened stepping off the small commuter plane. I had no idea what would transpire in the week that lay ahead, but I was certain I wanted to squeeze all that I could from the experience, reconnecting with my Warrior Woman, and allowing myself to be immersed in whatever adventures were on the horizon.

I roomed with a seasoned guide and master casting instructor who hailed from the Pacific Northwest. Chatting with her one evening, after returning on the float plane from another epic day wrangling coho salmon and dodging grizzly bears in the wilds of Alaska's backcountry, I asked her about her foray into fly fishing. She shared her journey of brilliantly navigating the male-dominated industry to pursue her goals related to guiding, instruction and leadership roles. She talked about overcoming obstacles and staying focused on her passion of bringing more women into the sport.

"I would love to do something similar," I told her, in an offhand way, not feeling the confidence of being able to pursue the level of badassery she exhibited.

"You'd be a great instructor!" she said encouragingly.

Instead of dismissing that accolade, I internalized it, letting her positive message take root. Her encouragement was enough to plant a seed that, over the next several years, would start to grow with reckless abandon.

When I arrived home from Alaska, I immediately booked another all-women's fly fishing trip to Kiritimati (better known as Christmas Island), an even more remote location, about 110 miles north of the equator, in the Central Pacific Ocean, where I could trade cold water rivers for warm saltwater flats.

Even before I realized fly fishing would become so integral to my healing journey, I knew there was something magical about it. I felt connected, aligned, and at peace when I allowed myself to just be. Be in the water. Be with the birds. Be part of something bigger than myself.

With COVID and my work at the VA hospital progressing, the trip to Christmas Island was indefinitely postponed. I should have been disappointed, but the news came as a relief. Anxiety and unease were creeping back into my world, and I debated if I was stable enough to travel across the world with a group of women I didn't know, be dropped off on a tiny, remote island, and stay, for a week, in a place I was unfamiliar with that had limited communications and no way to get off the island if things went off the rails. There was only one flight from Hawai'i, and one back there, every seven days. It felt very Gilligan's Island, and I wasn't sure I was up for that level of adventure when I was feeling depleted, sleep-deprived and on-edge.

What I yearned for was more of the quiet stillness that fly fishing provided, and the power of coming alongside women to feel connection and community. I no longer wanted to hold myself back from the things I knew God was asking me to do. With Christmas Island no longer on the horizon, I prayed for the next opportunity that felt a little safer but would still stretch me past my comfort zone.

As I scrolled through Facebook one evening, I came across a fly fishing outfitter in Montana that was offering a women-specific guide school. Guide school had not been on my radar, but I felt the glimmer, the notion, the pull that this was the next right move.

"You'd be a great instructor!" my former roommate had said.

That singular statement from a professional offered an idea for the possibility of something I couldn't yet fathom.

As I spent more time engaging in fly fishing activities, I'd found that being on a river or immersed in the saltwater flats, grappling with nature's elements, reading the movements of the wind, waves and currents, and just feeling the movement of water over my feet, created the centering and grounding that, ironically, helped steady me.

Fly fishing became a healing salve, forcing me to slow down and breathe.

It hadn't been my practice to stop, to reflect, to consider what slow and steady might look and feel like. For as long as I can remember, stopping, or even slowing down, felt too scary. Too uncertain. Too vulnerable. Too fraught with the what ifs that come when we choose trust over control.

What if I fail? What if I appear irresponsible? What if things don't work out the way I thought they would? What if people judge me? What if I'm the only one? What if I simply can't handle the thing that life throws at me next?

The problem with what-ifs is that life becomes lived on conjecture and speculation instead of firmly rooted in purpose, trust and mission.

At a very young age, my dad warned me against getting caught up in "what-ifs." He was unyielding in his assertion that we were not to use or even think about the term "what-if" because that would only lead to problems. As a 10-year-old, I'm not sure I really understood what Dad meant. Now, retrospectively, I wish I'd learned to heed his advice sooner because ruminating on the what-ifs is a large part of what kept me stuck and what caused my marriage to fail.

Pushing the what-ifs aside, I opted to take a chance and filled out the online interest form for the women's guide school. The following morning, Sweetwater called me and explained the program. After that conversation, I could feel the glimmer brighten, a hot, white heat in my belly, directing me to make the decision to take a week off work, fly to Montana and attend the course.

Glimmers That Simmer

"One can choose to go back towards safety or forward toward growth. Growth must be chosen, again and again, [as] fear must be overcome again and again."

- Abraham Maslow

I tend to get a ton of great ideas in the shower. They usually come at a time when I have no one to tell them to, and no way to write them down. So, I capture them in a bubble in my mind and cross my fingers that brain fog won't impede my ability to remember them in detail when I can solidify them on paper.

On this late summer morning, in the midst of COVID craziness, I was washing my hair when the inkling to create the Curbside Delivery Program hit me. With soapy bubbles dribbling down my face, I was formulating an idea where my team, and our now underutilized VA volunteers, would provide non-perishable food delivery to struggling veterans. Many of the VA's patients were on limited or fixed incomes and several had medical concerns that made public interactions during a wide-spread pandemic impossible. Routine and fundamental practices, like grocery store shopping, became problematic, creating an issue of food scarcity amongst an already fragile and vulnerable population. While no one was truly prepared for a universal pandemic, many older, or infirmed, veterans were having to make tough decisions. How does one choose to pay the electric bill or eat for the week? It was an insufferable position to be in.

When I arrived at the office, the curbside delivery idea was still pinging around in my captured bubble like a steel ball whizzing around a pinball table. I had mulled it over so many times in my head on the drive to work, I was spinning. I needed my team, and their reasonable and sound input to steady my thoughts and bring me back down to earth.

"So…" I began our staff meeting later that day, "I had an idea this morning that I want to run by you. This may sound a little crazy, but…"

Four people sat around a table that was piled high with the donations that kept coming in but remained in our office because we hadn't yet figured out a safe way to get them to the veterans who needed them most.

That was all about to change.

My staff looked at me, a mixture of skepticism, curiosity and intrigue lining their faces.

"What if we create a curbside delivery service?" I asked. "Kind of like Door Dash meets Amazon. We can deliver food, and other necessities to veterans at their homes."

I scanned the team, and the body posture indicated that, despite this being a seemingly off-the-wall request, maybe creativity would win out.

"Our volunteers can do the drop-offs," I continued, "and just deliver the items to veterans' doorsteps, or porches."

I looked around the table, searching for agreement, but heard nothing. So, I plodded on. "Veterans get what they need and volunteers get to do what they love to do. It's a win-win!"

Something I said ignited a fire in the team, and I could see the tide was beginning to shift. People were leaning in, legs uncrossing, pens making movement on previously blank paper. And then the words started to flow.

"I think it could work," one team member finally piped up. "We would need to get Social Work involved…"

"And Nutrition," another butted in.

"And I can look into the safety aspects for the volunteers," yet another inserted. "See what they would need to drive the vans and make the deliveries with zero contact."

Suddenly the room was buzzing with ideas and this initiative, that had started as a glimmer, was quickly transforming into a fully-fledged reality. It didn't take much time for the team to breathe life into the VA Curbside Delivery Program. Soon we were stuffing brown paper grocery bags full of non-perishable food and other critical items and sending them out to veterans who could use a hand-up. We created a process that was scalable and replicable and, after later becoming a VA "Diffusion of Excellence" winner for innovation, our program was adopted by other VA facilities around the nation as a best practice.

Days turned into a blur of paper bags (which I handled a lot better than paper gowns) and nature walks with Karen, Meatball, and Odin. On a warm August morning, just a few miles into our walk, my phone rang mid-way up the Ravenel Bridge.

"Hello?" I answered, a bit unsure because I usually didn't bother taking any calls when I was out walking. I wanted to remain fully present, soaking in the twinkles and sparkles of the sun's reflective rays which were bouncing off the water in-between the cement pillars that kept the bridge's spans stable and rooted.

"Hi. Is this Sue?" the male voice asked. My shoulders stiffened, just the tiniest little bit.

"It is." I still didn't recognize the number, so I was politely curt in my response.

"Hey. I'm calling from Sweetwater Guide School. In Montana." I never caught his name, but from his deadpan tone, it was clear that this phone call wasn't one he was excited to make. "We have a slight hiccup with the lodging situation that may affect our ability to offer the fly fishing guide school next week."

"What's the issue?" I asked, as my heart sank towards the bottom of the bridge. I was slated to leave in a few days and had been looking forward to plugging into the stillness of the river, and meeting other females who shared my love and interest in the sport.

"We are having some unexpected problems with accessing the lodge where we normally stay," he offered. "I am just calling to let you know that we are working on it, and I'll circle back in a few hours to let you know where things stand."

When we hung up, my heart sank. Christmas Island had been cancelled. Now this? I had prayed, asking for the Divine to guide my path and plug me into the things I needed as I moved forward. If guide school wasn't supposed to happen, why had I felt the urgency, the strong glimmer, directing me to apply? Why had I felt so strongly in the belief that I needed to go to Montana for this school, that I needed this education and encouragement to even consider the possibility of breathing life into that "You'd be a great instructor!" comment from Alaska that seeded itself deeply into my subconsciousness?

Standing here, with the Ravenel Bridge's traffic whizzing by, I was beginning to doubt the glimmers. What if the glimmers weren't real? Or what if it wasn't intuition that was guiding me, but, instead, false ideas providing false hope for things that would never come to fruition?

In a world that was already upside-down and chaotic, I wondered if it was all a farce. How ironic that fly fishing was supposed to heal, but, to gain the confidence to do it, I continued to feel like I was bumping up against roadblocks, which caused more frustration than healing.

"*What if my intuition is wrong?*" I asked myself. "*Am I not supposed to follow this path? Am I not allowed to meet other women who are into this?*"

I had become more and more involved with *Project Healing Waters*, attending meetings after work, forcing myself out of my comfort zone as I learned new skills, and even tried my hand at tying flies and building fly fishing rods. Soon, I was invited to attend single and multi-day fishing excursions, which became exhausting because I often was the only woman. I should have been used to being an anomaly. For years, I had stilted my authentic self to fit in with what I thought was expected of me. I'd learned to put my compassion, and softer parts of myself in a box - one that I could lock down and only allow certain people to access.

In fact, during the Coast Guard era, when I was part of the two percent of females that made up the officer corps, I would affectionately refer to myself as a *Gentle Fucking Flower*. Not because I wanted to be labeled as "soft" or "weak", but because I was desperately trying to figure out how to reconcile the feminine, compassionate parts of myself with those that had been programmed to show up with resolve and power. I wanted to be able to show all parts of myself, all parts of my Warrior Woman, but felt like only my sharp-around-the-edges parts were allowed to peek through.

I was driven by competency and forced myself to maintain a high level of professionalism so I would be taken seriously. I refused to allow myself to be vulnerable or open to diving deep into areas of my heart and soul that desperately needed tending. Instead, I remained stalwart and appeared strong, assertive, decisive, determined and, at times, aggressive. Some might have even considered me to be bitchy. I'd been indoctrinated into believing that showing emotion, vulnerability or even compassion equated to weakness. And a display of weakness meant that I wouldn't be successful or recognized as someone who could lead, inspire and prosper. I worked too hard to have a seat at the table, to have my voice heard. So, sacrificing these parts of myself seemed, at the time, like a reasonable risk.

I was absolutely by-the-book and learned to lean into being one way in my professional life, and quite a bit different in my personal affairs. So much so that my crew had given me the secret moniker, *Battle Axe*.

Just like a starfish, I kept the soft, vulnerable, squishy parts of my underbelly hidden because it was too risky, both professionally and personally, to be judged for being too compassionate, too kind, too vulnerable, too authentic. I didn't want to provide any fuel that could be used to create more misperceptions, stereotypes and narrow-minded thinking about the softness and feebleness of women. So, I rarely allowed myself the grace to be imperfect, weak or vulnerable. And I never, ever showed those aspects of myself in public.

Now, as the lone female in the fly fishing group, I found it hard to fully connect with the other participants because of my emotional baggage. I truly believed I was alone in my struggle to figure out what my feminine side could look and feel like because

I had been marginalized and stilted as I was forced to amalgamate to male-dominated work cultures. I had never been a victim, but I felt defeated for so, so long. I had been certain that every other woman on the planet knew how to manage stress, how to find a reasonable work-life balance, and how to avoid being pushed past her limits. For years I was convinced that I just needed to be stronger, tougher and smarter to fight the mental health battle and win. I was certain that all it would take was grit, tenacity and perseverance to get rid of the depression, anxiety and PTSD so I could move on and live my life like "normal" people.

"*Maybe I'm reading too much into this,*" I thought to myself, trying to shift the internal narrative away from the catastrophic and closer to minor annoyance with this unexpected speed bump. This was progress.

I wanted to feel like going (or not going) to Montana didn't matter. Yet, I knew it did. In my soul, I felt a pull beckoning me to head West and I knew this experience would force me to push past my own fears of inadequacy and incompetence.

"*There's no way I'm not going,*" I assured myself, then turned the conversation upward. "God," I said out loud, "I asked You for a solution. You gave me this opportunity. You put this in front of me. So, how are You going to just take it away? Is this not what I'm meant to be pursuing?"

The phone rang again.

"Sue," came the same male voice over the receiver, "we got it figured out."

Tiny butterflies of excitement, mixed with uncertainty, flittered inside my belly, confirming that the glimmers were real. I was fixated on my needs, my wants, my desired outcomes for the upcoming week. But I would come to find out was God wanted so much more. He was playing the long game and He knew that, by sending me to Montana, I would start to connect the dots between the importance of establishing a supportive community, the correlation between nature and healing and what these critical factors would mean to me later in being able to share my story, my struggle, my triumphs and my growth in authentic and impactful ways.

"We've changed locations, so you'll need to fly into Billings."

"Ok," I said, knowing it would be easy to switch the ticket.

Two days later, I boarded a plane, headed for Billings, Montana, and whatever adventures awaited me in Big Sky Country.

Fishy Pants

"There is something infinitely healing in the repeated refrains of nature – the assurance that dawn comes after night, and spring after winter."

- Rachel Carson

I arrived in Billings on a late-night flight and overnighted in a rustic motel near the airport. Early the next morning, I made my way back to the arrivals terminal to begin my Montana adventure. I saw a line of trucks and drift boats parked just outside baggage claim and found the young woman who would be one of the guides leading us through the week. Gathering my luggage, I followed her to her SUV, a combination of excitement and trepidation welling up inside me. As I noticed the fiberglass boat, with two oars, attached to the vehicle's hitch, the reality of this adventure barreled into me at full force.

Soon, I would be in the rower's seat, with those oars in my hands, making my way down the Yellowstone River. I'd be navigating boulders, downed trees, swift water and the unpredictable twists and turns that only a living, wild river can provide.

As the SUV pulled out of the arrivals area and onto the road which would take us to the Airbnb that the outfitter booked last minute to alleviate the lodging situation, my guide/driver gestured with open palms to the blue sky just on the other side of the windshield.

"Welcome to Montana!" she proclaimed. "The last best place."

I turned my head to glance out of my passenger side window. I couldn't see much in the darkness when I arrived the previous evening. But here, with the immense August sky illuminating every crevice of the surrounding landscape, I was absolutely awestruck by the jagged edges of the sandstone bluffs, streaked with rust-red iron glints, rising up from the floor of the Yellowstone Valley. As we continued our journey, the mountains that once were distant came into view, standing like silent sentinels that had watched over this sacred landscape for millennia. The Yellowstone River snaked through craggy banks, as the golden leaves of autumn blazed along its trail. This was wild, rugged country, dotted with working ranches and cattle that made everything vivid, raw and unfiltered.

I took in the colors and the varying backdrops, and the stress I typically carried with me, like an overloaded purse, started to diminish. I was filled with a type of gratitude I wasn't familiar with. It was a feeling of thankfulness to be part of something that was so much bigger than myself and hope that the glimmer that had directed me to sign up for this course would prove to me that this was more than just a trip to Montana.

We arrived at the Airbnb about an hour-and-a-half later and, as we parked in the circular dirt driveway of the log cabin, my heart started racing. We had found our way down a long dirt road, littered by wildflowers and the occasional rustic cabin tucked in behind tall grasses and fences. I was excited to meet our group, which consisted of eight women, all coming together for a week of learning, personal growth and fly fishing. Each of us brought with us our own story and our own reasons for being there.

The SUV came to a halt, and I grabbed my gear, which included rods, reels, waders and boots, and climbed the steep staircase leading up to the log cabin's front door. Once inside, someone directed me to my room, and I opened the large oak door to find an expansive, well-appointed area that included an en-suite bathroom and a private balcony. I wasn't sure how I got so lucky, but appreciated the space to relax. I put my bags down, unpacked a few key items, and then headed back down the hall to the kitchen, where some of my classmates had gathered.

"Does anyone want to go for a walk?" I asked after we had completed our formal introductions. Karen's friendship brought me many lessons, and the simple act of walking and talking was a gift from her that I coveted. We were still waiting on a handful of ladies to arrive and had some time before the first scheduled event. Walking seemed like a great option to pass the time and get to know these gals.

"Sure!" one woman replied with a slight Kentucky twang. "Me too!" chimed in another.

"Awesome," I replied, and out the door we went.

As we walked, the three of us chatted about our fly fishing experiences, our reasons for convening in Montana, and our hopes for the week. Sydney, the youngest of the cohort and the owner of the Kentucky drawl, mentioned that she was headed to school at Murray State to start her course of studies in Earth and Environmental Science. She was an avid fly fisherwoman with a heart for adventure. Liking almost all things outdoors, including horseback riding and hiking, I would come to find out that Sydney didn't really have an interest in fly fishing at first, because she thought it would be difficult. However, her mom, also with a penchant for adventure, invited Sydney to fly fish with her one day and, agreeing to put aside her hesitation and give it a whirl, Sydney found herself immersed in the river, hunting for brook trout.

It was hard to believe that someone who would turn out to be so proficient as a fly angler experienced hesitation at the onset. But, one thing I would come to love about Sydney, was that despite any hesitation, she was decisive and persistent. She was willing to put her uncertainties aside to try new things because, for her, the adventure of it all was the payoff.

Over the next week, Sydney would show up for class in her brightly colored leggings, with different fish patterns splashed across their fabrics. I'd never seen any pants with bold, fishy prints like these, and my curiosity got the best of me.

"Sydney," I approached her one morning over coffee. "What's the deal with the pants?"

"Oh," she said as she glanced down to see which ones she was wearing. "They are meant to mimic different fish species."

I was flabbergasted that someone could sport such a shockingly bold pants pattern, but Sydney wore them with confidence and self-assurance. I loved that about her. Sydney had no fear.

I once had been like Sydney, moving through the world so easily, without all the fear, without all of the relentless insecurities weighing me down. Fearless, tenacious, bold. Where had the turning point been where I had lost myself and the fierceness that was once a trademark attribute? Was it after I left the Coast Guard, and tried to balance the dissonance between being a *Battle Axe* and a *Gentle Fucking Flower*? Was it when I had lost my path, my purpose and a dream to chase? Or was it a slow burn that was years in the unravelling?

I thought about pivotal moments when things had notably

shifted and changed. My mind flitted back to the cool Panama City Beach, Florida morning, in November of 2012. Ironman Florida flags were staked in the sand, moving lazily in the pre-dawn breeze. I stood on the beach, swim cap holding my dark locks in place, goggles firmly affixed, ready to shield my eyes from the saltwater, as I took several long breaths, waiting for the announcer to call my heat.

People were already in the water, battling an incoming tide that was creating chaos about 100 meters from our starting position on the beach. Waves were forming, crashing, forming again, as swimmers were riding over them like dolphins, towards a sky that was just starting to let the morning alpenglow peek through.

"Shit," I muttered under my breath as J.P. stood next to me, asking if I was ready to go. "I think so," is what I answered, looking up into his eyes with all the confidence I could muster.

When I signed up for the Ironman triathlon a year earlier, I had immediate buyer's remorse, thinking to myself, "*There's no way. There's just no way I can do this. This is ridiculous.*" But a glimmer had urged me out of the kitchen in the condo where we were staying, and over to the event grounds the morning after my friends had completed it in 2011. Something deep inside me told me that I needed to compete in the following year's event. It made no sense, but following glimmers seldom does.

"You've got this," J.P. said to me as he gave me a quick hug. "Now, go do it! And don't forget about the kids!"

His comment grounded me. I had spent the last eleven months fundraising for children of incarcerated parents, which kept me motivated and focused during my two-a-day training sessions. I sent out social media posts, asking for donations, and raised a couple of thousand dollars to benefit the charity that served these at-risk children.

I gave J.P. one last hug, took another deep breath and entered the water. The temperature had been just cool enough to allow participants to don wetsuits, and I opted to take advantage of the extra buoyancy. I walked out, feeling the gritty sand between my toes, until the depth overtook my 5'2" frame and I had no choice but to swim. The waves I had been watching all morning continued on their relentless rhythm of building, breaking, and carrying themselves back out to sea with a strong undercurrent.

"*Stroke, stroke, stroke, breathe,*" I told myself as I counted my cadence in my head. "*In line, just like a zipper. Stroke, stroke, stroke, breathe.*" I could feel the waves pushing against me, sucking up all the advancing motion I was trying to gain.

I had remembered that one of my friends, who had successfully completed this same Ironman the previous year, lived by the moniker, "Slow is steady, steady is fast." Now I knew what she meant.

"*COME ON SUE,*" my inside voice screamed in my head. "*PUSH!*"

I swam a little faster.

"*Stroke…stroke…stroke…breathe.*" Each stroke slicing through the incessant waves, trying to create forward momentum in the messiness of it all.

After several minutes, I stilled my strokes and looked around, trying to gain a clearer picture of my course and distance from shore. As I treaded water, I could see that the shoreline was only four or five football fields distance behind me. My confidence deflated as I realized I was literally struggling to go nowhere fast.

And then I pictured those kids, living without the stability of parents and who needed to be given a chance to be loved. This had nothing to do with crossing a finish line, and everything to do with making good on a promise I had made that would nurture, educate and protect these vulnerable children.

I put my goggled face back in the water, threw my left arm forward, and began to stroke with power and persistence, pulling me past the waves and into the calmer waters.

It took me 1:59:20 to complete the 2.4-mile swim distance, and another 7:39:02 to finish the 112-mile bike ride and 6:16:57 to walk the full 26.2-mile marathon.

"Sue Kerver..." the voice boomed over the speakers as I crossed the finish line, almost 17 hours later, "YOU. ARE. AN. IRONMAN!"

In the darkness of the evening, with crowds of cheering observers, I realized what I had just done. I crossed that finish line after 16:30:15 of grit, sweat, tenacity and tears, fulfilling the promise I'd made to myself, to others, to those kids.

I had achieved my impossible.

Despite all of the hardship that had come after this pivotal moment, I never stopped believing that progress could happen. Yet, I had let fear get in the way. As I came to know Sydney for her quiet confidence and willingness to try most things, I wondered where Ironman Sue had gone. Where was that part of me - the one who was like Sydney and wasn't hesitant to dive in, because she knew bigger things were at risk if she didn't push past the uncomfortable? Where was the woman who believed that being open to the possibilities that are just beyond what we see and know, helps us become limitless?

I had done so many hard things. So, why couldn't I muster up the courage to do something as simple as showing up in fun and fantastic fishy pants, like my new friend Sydney?

I wondered if the level of confidence that comes from a bottle had been stripped from me because I chose sobriety over satiety. Had I lost my capability to do hard things because I was no longer fueled by liquid courage? Or was I simply realizing that I had become disillusioned because nothing I did, or achieved, ever felt like it was enough? Where had my Warrior Woman gone, and what would I need to do to get her back? I was realizing that it was time to stop searching for a level of acceptance and perfectionism that was unrealistic and, instead, lean into embracing my faults, imperfections, and insecurities because these are the things that allowed me to show up authentically in the first place.

There was something so real about having to acknowledge that I had lost parts of myself, and in that loss, the devastation of it all had torn my world apart. Now I was seeding a new path, one where change could be revitalizing if I chose to let go of things that no longer served me and invite in those things that were in alignment with my values and beliefs.

As the week progressed, so did our fly fishing skills. We all took turns rowing drift boats down the churning Yellowstone River, where huge rocks created whitewater rapids, and cliff faces jetted out of the river's bends.

"We were told that we were going to be on like a soft, slow-moving river," Sydney reminded me years later as we reminisced about our guide school experience on the podcast. "And then we ended up being just dropped in headfirst. That was a great experience though. I mean, there's nothing better than doing that."

Quiet confidence.

Seven days later, after refining my cast, successfully, and not so successfully, netting a variety of species and learning how to catch and release trout by keeping them wet and minimizing their time on the end of our lines, I headed back to Charleston, ready for my next challenge.

I recognized that if I could be successful on the river, doing something that, even a week before, seemed somewhat inaccessible, I could find other ways to reclaim my authority. I could invite my Warrior Woman back in and ask Her to help me reinvent this version of Sue.

It was time for me to let go of the emotional baggage that was weighing me down and start to pursue the things that were on my heart. It was time for me to reengage with purpose. And it was time for me to go buy a pair of fishy pants and wear those on the river, and to the grocery store, and wherever else I damn well pleased as an act of power, self-love, and self-confidence.

Odin's Little Red Wagon

"We must be willing to let go of the life we planned so as to have the life that is waiting for us."
- Joseph Campbell

I thought reclaiming my authority would be easy. I believed I could will myself into feeling calm by forcibly reframing negative thoughts into positive ones and staying consistent with exercise and sobriety.

However, despite pouring my energy into all the things that had worked before, including morning prayer, journaling, gratitude, and spending time exploring the Low Country's cypress-tupelo swamps, maritime forests, and beaches, I could feel the high I had been riding since Montana begin to dissipate. I was having a hard time staving off unwelcomed emotions, and the familiar feelings of depression and anxiety started creeping in. I was shuttering inward and shutting down, just like the COVID world around me.

Karen and I were walking regularly but, even with her joyous company, my inner peace was starting to fray. Meatball relished our long jaunts across the Ravenel Bridge and, when we opted for the beach instead, Odin came along. Odin's aging hips and joints made it hard for him to walk longer distances, so I bought a bright red wagon, with sturdy offroad tires and a reinforced steel frame, so he could have a place to comfortably, and happily, sit as I lugged him through thc sand.

My conversations with Karen grew deeper and one afternoon, in the heat of the South Carolina sun, walking past the Cold War Memorial near Patriot's Point, I offered her my truth.

"So," I nonchalantly started, not entirely sure of how I wanted to present this info, "I'm not exactly doing ok." It was a simple, yet effective statement.

Karen slowed, turning towards me, grabbing a glance at my face to ascertain the severity of my statement.

"What do you mean? Like with COVID?"

"Kind of," I admitted, "but I think it's more than that. I think I might be falling off the cliff."

In my mind, that statement made complete sense but, for Karen, without the previous context of paper gowns and fallen crowns, I realized further explanation was needed.

"It's just that, after I got divorced, I went through a really serious meltdown. It was bad. I…I just wasn't sure if I was going to make it."

She turned to look at me again but said nothing.

"I'm starting to feel like that again. And it scares the hell out of me."

There it was. That singular admission that I had fallen once and was absolutely terrified that a second time was imminent. Despite COVID, my daily routine stayed constant and, in a world that felt upside down, I appreciated the stability and structure of having a few small things I could control because everything else, including work, felt like plates I was spinning, trying to keep them all from crashing to the ground.

I worked for a stout man, with a large belly and an even larger personality. I had privately nicknamed him *The Mayor* because he had a propensity to shake hands and engage with everyone he met when he did his daily hospital rounds.

One afternoon, as it neared 5 p.m., The Mayor summoned me to his small office. For the two years I worked for him, I noticed his modus operandi was to pull me in towards the end of the workday and have these types of in-depth conversations. I never figured out if this was his passive aggressive way of making me stay later than my normal working hours, or if he was just too busy during conventional hours and he'd allocated time near the end of each workday to tackle issues he wanted me to weigh in on. Either way, it was an inconsiderate power play that I began to deeply resent.

On this particular afternoon, The Mayor wanted to chat about women's health because the hospital had talked about expanding services for their female patients. He was seeking input from both the female patient perspective, as well as from the provider perspective and I met some of those criteria. Except, as it turned out, the conversation turned into more of a one-way monologue than a two-way discourse, and my input really wasn't wanted.

"Mammograms," he said with an air of aloofness as I sat across from him, staring at the stacks of unfiled papers that were haphazardly stacked atop his small, metal desk. "We need to get a mammogram machine."

"There's a lot more to women's health than just breast exams," I countered.

We had been through this dance before. The one where he would ask for my input as a performative exercise so he could say he solicited feedback from female veterans. I never felt he had any intention of actually using the nuggets he gleaned because, it seemed, once he had his head wrapped around an idea, any further opportunities for collaboration, input or thoughts were moot. But here I was, as the clock ticked closer to quitting time, with the opportunity to fulfill the promise I'd made to advocate for women veterans. This seemed like a way to do that, so I pressed on.

"I think we need to be thinking about hormone testing, perimenopause, change-of-life, pregnancy, post-partum depression," I said. With my ongoing mental health concerns, I was convinced some of my dis-ease could be attributed to hormonal shifts. The problem was, I couldn't find a healthcare provider who would listen to me, or who knew enough about these issues, to make me feel seen, heard, and understood. And these resources certainly were not available within my local VA healthcare system.

"Maybe," he responded in a non-committal tone.

"If we are going to talk about women's health," I continued, "we need to talk about the totality of a woman. There's a lot more to us than breast tissue."

He shifted in his chair, his blonde comb-over moving ever so slightly, as he repositioned himself into a spot of authority.

"Look, I agree with you that mammograms are important," I said. "And it's a lot of hassle to go out to another location to get one done. But there are other things that women need that are equally important."

I thought back to my time in Ethiopia, and the lack of reproductive options, the absence of adequate healthcare, the minimization of women, and the removal of their voice, power and choice. For years after returning to the United States, I ruminated over cultural beliefs that condoned genital mutilation as an acceptable method for controlling women's sexual authority and wondered if a society could evolve when the predominant belief system centered around using women merely as vessels to create offspring, cook, clean, fetch water and attend to all matters of the home.

"I know women veterans who have had issues getting pregnant and want help with infertility and their menstrual cycles," I continued. "There are some who have had post-partum depression but there are no services to assist with that. And, even with the pregnancy, women must go to a different facility to have the child because the VA doesn't offer birthing options or pre- or post-natal care. We don't even have comprehensive gynecological services."

He continued to fidget. Back and forth. Back and forth. His beefy hand ran through his golden locks, absently pulling the weight of his bangs back from his forehead. Was he uncomfortable talking about menstruation, or was he just uncomfortable that I was holding the line?

"That's not really what we do," he said. Now I understood it was the latter, making me wonder why we were even having this conversation. His cheeks flushed, and he seemed frustrated to be in the position where he needed to inform me of the VA's mission because, clearly, that was something I should have already known. I was well versed in what the VA did and didn't provide, and thought my knowledge and understanding of these things could provide a different perspective. From my lived experience, I knew the VA didn't even begin to scratch the surface of meeting the needs of the women who had valiantly served this country. Yet, here I was, staring down the barrel of a double shotgun, in the form of yet another male who purportedly knew more about my body than I did, trying to defend the obvious. It was exasperating.

"If the goal is to expand women's health, we need to lean into hormones and menopause and all the things that are significant and unique to being a woman." I made my point. Again.

"We need a mammogram machine."

That was his answer. End of conversation. I had just wasted an hour having one of the most awkward conversations of my life, trying to be honest and authentic as we talked about ta-tas and lady bits, and here we were, back at square one, circling back to the conclusion that he'd formed before we even talked. It was so short-sighted and it infuriated me that another male authority figure felt emboldened to show me, in real time, that my opinions, my ideas, my voice were not valued. I wasn't valued. This interaction was representative of all the times I had been shut down, not seen, not heard, not respected. This narrative had been a constant companion most of my adult life, and I was exhausted. I was fed-up, always trying to prove to him, and to all who had come before him, that the possibilities could be bigger, if only they would listen.

Sitting there in the airless office, I glanced down at my watch. It was now well after 5 p.m. I should have been walking Meatball and Odin on the beach instead of engrossed in an argument I would never win. And something inside of me snapped.

"Why did you even ask me then?" I barked, my voice rising an octave as I stood up from the hard office chair. Tears hovered just on the bottom of my eyelids, and I could feel that quiet unhinging that usually starts in my belly and quickly works its way up to my throat. I knew a panic attack was lurking.

Turning from him, I stormed out of the closet-like office, down the hall, trying to escape as feelings of worthlessness and insignificance loomed. I couldn't let him see me fall apart. I prided myself on being professional, and this was one of the first times I could remember that I showed a noticeable chink in my armor.

I thought about the conversation I'd had with Karen, admitting that I was in the express lane to full-blown burnout mode, on my way to another serious breakdown. I knew I had to do something, but I also knew that the coping mechanisms that had worked before were no longer effective. I had to adapt, like the starfish, and find ways to regenerate, even of renewal came in incremental spurts.

It was time to put myself first, so I sought out an agreement which allowed me to work from an alternate location for a couple of weeks. In early October, I drove to my sister's house in Texas, and, after work, attended my nephews' baseball games, practiced yoga at a local studio and walked miles on Austin's Greenbelt. Everything began to normalize as I gained some space from my toxic work environment and re-established a personal flow which allowed me to peek back out of the tough shell that I had crawled into. I also applied for, and was accepted to, the Mission Continues' Women Veterans Leadership Program, which was scheduled to commence in December. I was excited for a new challenge, and a way to connect with other female leaders who had shared experiences, hoping it would be as profound and empowering as my all-women's fly fishing week in Montana.

When I arrived back home a few weeks later, I called Karen so we could resume our walking schedule. After work, Karen and I would pack up the dogs and comb the beaches, feeling safe during COVID in a way only the outdoors provided.

"Here," she said one afternoon as she pulled a grayish garment from the back seat of her car. A sweatshirt, with the word "FRIENDS" emblazoned across the front, flapped in the sea breeze and I noticed that Karen had lovingly cropped the arms and torso to fit Odin's front legs and chest area. "The wind gets pretty chilly," she continued. "So, I just want to make sure he's warm."

It wasn't lost on me that Karen had provided a snuggly sweatshirt from a TV series that elevated the importance of having people in your life whom you could unequivocally count on. She slipped the sweatshirt over Odin's head, pulling his arthritic legs into the warmth of the fleece-lined garment and aligned the "FRIENDS" logo along the center of his belly. His aging brown eyes twinkled as she continued to dress him, pulling the hood up over his floofy white ears, and cinching the hoodie's laces tight around his fully gray face.

"All set," she uttered as she finished up and inspected her handiwork. And, with one last pat to his head, we were on our way. I grabbed the handle of the red wagon with both hands and pulled his 80-pound body down the length of the boardwalk and into the sand. Meatball loped along beside us, smelling the sea oats and tall green grass. It was always so much work to pull that little red wagon through shifting sands, but I knew that this walk was just as important for Odin as it was for me. I'd wished that every male in my life was as kind, as gentle, as loving as my senior Golden Retriever. Somehow though, I kept being placed in positions where experience proved the opposite.

A few weeks later, as I sat in my office after my team departed at 4 p.m., I heard a key turn the lock of the large glass double doors. The small creak indicated that they were opening, and someone entered the office space, where I sat alone, engrossed in a phone conversation. I asked my team members to lock the heavy glass doors when they left for the day, because it made me feel a little safer being in there by myself. And, aside from the security and cleaning crews, very few people had keys to unlock them.

"Hold on a sec," I said into the headset as I put the phone on mute to find out who was there. "Hello?" I called out. "Who's there?"

The Mayor responded with a quipped acknowledgement. I didn't think too much of The Mayor coming into the space, and figured he was looking for clothing, or hygiene products, or some other donated item that was needed for a patient he was assisting. But then, I heard him try the locks on each one of the cubicles, shuffling his large body from one office door to the next until he found one that opened.

"Is there something you need?" I called out from my office. I didn't want to get up from my desk to engage with him if I didn't need to, remembering all the times that late day communications resulted in staying far longer than I intended. And, my caller was still on hold.

"I'm all set," he responded, his voice coming from inside the office that was across the room and cattycorner from where I sat.

I could hear shuffling and then moments of louder huffing and puffing.

"What are you doing?" I asked, trying to solve a complex puzzle without all of the pieces.

"I'm running late," he responded. "I just needed a place to change my clothes."

Before I could begin to process what he said, he emerged from the tiny cubicle, closed the door behind him, and exited the office space through the double glass doors from whence he came.

"I, uh, I'm going to have to call you back," I stuttered into my phone as I heard the glass doors click shut.

He was gone, and I was speechless.

"*What in the hell just happened?*" I asked myself, as I relayed the events of the past few minutes.

On the drive home, on my walk on the beach, and throughout the remainder of my evening routine, I couldn't stop thinking about what had happened. I spent the night wondering if I was being too sensitive and spinning myself up about something that was inconsequential. I never actually saw him change his clothes. So, maybe I was overreacting?

The next morning, I spoke with a trusted female ally in a senior leadership position. I was looking for counsel, clarity and direction. We walked across the street, stopping in a sheltered area where she could smoke without the prying eyes of patients or colleagues.

"Do I confront him?" I asked. I was afraid that speaking up could lead to retribution, and I was questioning my own judgement. "I mean – was it really that egregious? It's not like I could see him. He was behind a closed door."

"Yes, you absolutely need to say something," she affirmed as she took a deep drag of her cigarette. "That kind of behavior is not ok. Sue, he's your superior." She paused, exhaling sharply and flicking the ash to the sidewalk. "If you don't say something, I will."

"*Maybe she's right,*" I considered, as I walked back to my office, trying to air out the residual stank of stale smoke that clung to my work pants. I hated the smell of cigarettes. The odor was invasive, holding onto anything that would capture and keep its scent. I'd smoked for years and, after quitting, I couldn't stand the smell. "*Maybe I do need to say something.*"

As I continued my walk, I extended my path, wanting to spend a bit more time in contemplative consideration. I wanted to understand why I felt out-of-sorts. After a few minutes of processing, I concluded that The Mayor's stunt deeply violated my boundaries that I relied on to create trust and safety. It opened old wounds that I'd spent years trying to heal and I knew that the only way to control the damage was to confront the issue.

"I need to talk to you," I said, as I knocked on The Mayor's office door later that afternoon. Even after my formidable conclusion on the walk back to my office, it took hours to summon up the courage to have the conversation.

I entered his office, closing the door only part of the way, because I wanted to balance the need for privacy with my need to be in a space that was psychologically safe. "What happened last night made me feel really uncomfortable."

"What are you talking about?" he asked, keeping his eyes trained on the computer screen instead of in my direction.

Was he serious? I could feel the heat rise to my cheeks, as I tried to keep my rage under control. "I'm talking about the fact that you came into a shared office space and changed your clothes."

"So?" he questioned, now changing tactics, looking directly into my eyes. His piercing glare told me that I'd lost my mind. "I was in a walled cubicle, behind a closed door. You're making too much out of this." Then he turned back to his computer screen, clearly done with this conversation. And, done with me.

"*Be professional Sue,*" I reminded myself. But anger was overtaking my sensibilities.

"I'm NOT making too much out of this." I leaned into the chair I was standing behind, steadying myself as I searched for my next statement. "It was after hours. No one except me was in that space." My voice was rising, along with the anxiety that was creeping in. "You should have expressed better judgement."

"I didn't have time," he said curtly as he looked back in my direction. He placed both hands on the metal desk, looking like he was preparing to rise in case things got too heated. "I was late," he said matter-of-factly, the contriteness of his tone making me feel like I was gaslighting myself. "Sue, I already told you," he said, clearly ready to put an end to this conversation, "You are making way too much out of this situation. It's no big deal."

That was it. That was the straw that broke me. The slight unravelling I'd been feeling turned into a massive fissure. I was pissed and was NOT going to let him tell me that my safety and well-being were "no big deal."

This conversation showed me that my perceptions didn't matter. But I knew they did. So, in an unprecedented act of self-love and self-preservation, I filed for Family Medical Leave Act (FMLA) and decided to take an extended absence from work to attend to the safety and well-being that The Mayor had so quickly dismissed. I wanted to seek treatment for the anxiety and crippling panic attacks that I'd been experiencing since I got back from Austin. They had been increasing in intensity and frequency, an external manifestation of the internal storm that was brewing because of COVID and this workplace toxicity. Even though I was terrified of falling off the cliff, and yellow paper gowns haunted my dreams, I knew that I had the grit, the tenacity, and the power to choose differently. It was time to unleash the fishy pants.

On a chilly November morning, with the paperwork filed and no real explanation to my team as to why I was leaving, I packed up Meatball and Odin and his little red wagon and headed back to Texas. Deciding to walk out on my crew, at a time when COVID had made things so uncertain, felt self-absorbed and self-serving. Yet, retrospectively, it was hugely courageous.

Leaving was so much harder than I had anticipated. I didn't know what would happen once I got to Austin, and this decision felt like I was positioning myself to abandon everything that I had spent years building. I was silently saying goodbye to my home, my job, my friends, and a coastal lifestyle that I had come to love.

As I pulled out of my driveway, watching my little grey cottage, with its bright yellow door, disappear in my rearview mirror, my breath caught. I drove for a few minutes after turning out of my neighborhood, wondering if I had locked the front and back doors. I was pretty sure I had, but, just in case, I turned my truck around and headed back to the house to do a security check. I was right – they were locked. Five minutes later, I was back on the road, again headed towards Austin. I hadn't driven a few miles when another nagging thought creeped in and throttled my rational brain. "*Did I leave the sink running?*" I envisioned all my movements that morning in reverse order, trying to create an image strong enough to convince me that I didn't need to turn around and drive back home to check.

I failed.

So, I made a U-turn just before crossing the Ravenel Bridge and drove the four miles back home to make sure the faucet in the kitchen wasn't running.

It wasn't.

After the second false start, I forced myself to keep driving despite the flood of invasive thoughts that kept creeping in. As Charleston grew dim in my rearview mirror, I spent the next 1,227 miles wondering if I had made the right decision. Every time I questioned myself, and the path that was unfolding before me, God showed up with tiny glimmers that kept me moving forward.

I thought about the Curbside Delivery program and its successful adoption across the nation. I thought about choosing to go to Alaska by myself, and all the new friends I had met. I thought about how I had said yes to Karen's invitations to walk, and the incredible friendship we had forged. I thought about guide school, and Sydney, and saying yes to the online resiliency workshops that addressed MST in safe and creative ways.

These monumental events had all started as glimmers – tiny moments, fueled by nothing more than gut feelings, that continued to light my path and drive me forward. And, despite the uncertainty of each of these situations, I was coming to understand that there was a direct correlation between my saying yes, even when things didn't always make sense, and monumental shifts that occurred when I listened to God's intuitive love language, trusting in the Divine Interventions.

A Little Wonder Woman In All Of Us

"Sometimes you can't see what you are learning until you come out the other side."

– Wonder Woman

As I drove across the country, I started to let go of the guilt that had plagued me since leaving Charleston, recognizing that sometimes waving the white flag, and asking for help, came with the uncomfortability of change. And, as much as I wanted to feel grounded, stable and rooted, I needed something different, so I had to be open to receiving whatever different looked like on this leg of my journey.

It didn't take me long after arriving in Austin to assemble a care team, which included a psychiatrist, a psychologist, a naturopathic doctor, a nutritionist, an acupuncturist, and yoga teachers. I also spoke with the VA about alternatives to psychotropic medications, because, after another unsuccessful attempt to stay on the Lexapro that the hospital had prescribed three years earlier, I knew that pills would never be my answer. The VA suggested Transcranial Magnetic Stimulation (TMS), which I hoped would be a viable, noninvasive solution for lifting the major depression that had set in. It wouldn't resolve the PTSD, but I knew I had to start somewhere.

I didn't know much about TMS, but what I did know was that I wouldn't fully commit to it until I could get more information. I wanted to fully explore the potential side effects and obtain a deeper understanding of how the science actually worked. Ironically, I was terrified to go down the internet rabbit hole looking for answers to these questions so, instead, I asked my sister to do it for me. As Sarah tackled the research aspect, I poured myself into investigating nearby TMS clinics and making phone calls to inquire about availability. There was a facility with high customer satisfaction ratings about 10 miles north of Sarah's place, and they were able to see me for the initial consultation.

I asked Sarah to accompany me so I would have a second set of ears as they explained the treatment protocols. "I'm terrified," I confided as we sat at her well-loved kitchen table the night before the appointment. "I don't know if it's brain fog or anxiety, but I can't process all this. And I have no idea how I'm going to even wrap my head around the TMS stuff."

"Don't worry," she assured me. "We've got this."

The following morning, we pulled into the parking lot in front of a nondescript, creamy brick building which was tucked in the back of an affluent neighborhood. Walking inside, the interior matched my suspicions, and I could tell this facility was a relatively new building, which brought a little bit of comfort.

There weren't any other patients, so it didn't take long for the tech to greet us and start showing us the ropes. We left the main waiting area and walked down a short hallway, to one of two treatment rooms. As we stepped inside, my eyes were drawn to something from a sci-fi movie. It had the likeness of a dental chair but attached to the left side of it was a computer and a monitor.

"This is the treatment chair," the tech noted, motioning to the only obvious piece of furniture in the room.

From Sarah reporting back on her internet research, I had gathered bits and pieces of how TMS was supposed to work. But I was here to get the whole story. "How does it work exactly?" I asked skeptically, eyeing the machinery up and down, wondering how this contraption would alleviate my depressive moods, release me from my intrusive thoughts, and build the bridge back to normalcy that had been washed away in the torrent of recent events.

"Well," the tech said as her hand reached for a headpiece with a built-in magnet, "this piece right here," she pointed at the large silver magnet that was attached to the headgear with a couple of screws, "will be used to tap the outside of your head, near your prefrontal cortex. It's meant to wake up your brain. It's like bringing it out of a long winter's hibernation." I had grown up in Colorado, so I knew winters could be variable. Some were excruciatingly long, while others were short lived. My brain's hibernation was definitely trending towards the former.

"Huh," I muttered under my breath, that word expressing both fear and uncertainty.

"And how long does it take?" I asked. "I mean, to bring my brain out of hibernation?"

"Over the course of the next six weeks, you'll need to come in every day, except on the weekends. Each session will take an hour and, after that, it'll take three more weeks for us to titrate you down and complete the entire protocol."

I was not thrilled to have to sit in that chair for an hour a day for the next two months. But I had made a promise to myself. Whatever it took. As I reminded myself this treatment had been well tested, it was FDA approved, and Sarah assured me her internet research hadn't shown any signs that it would melt my brain.

"And what about the anxiety?" I inquired, rooting around for more clarity.

"We will do bi-lateral stimulation, meaning we will align the magnet on the left side first and then do a shorter protocol on the right side as the second part to your daily treatment."

"*Twice the fun,*" I sarcastically thought to myself.

"How do you even know where it goes?" Sarah asked. It seemed like such an elementary question, but surely, I thought, there had to be some science behind this.

"That's a great question," the tech noted. "We will have Sue come in and go through the set-up process before the treatment protocol even starts. Once we determine the best placement on either side, we can save that info in the computer which ensures we have the right alignment and set up every single time."

It was like plugging a latitude and longitude into a GPS and making micro adjustments until the exact location was locked in. Then saving it to your navigation so all you had to do was hit "home" without much fanfare.

Leaving the office, I still wasn't convinced. "Hey," I turned to Sarah, "would you be willing to do some additional internet research? Maybe look to see, for sure, that it's not going to make things way worse? This whole thing is freaking me out."

We both knew that once I started to go down the internet rabbit hole, it would put me into an irreversible tailspin of anxiety and angst, which likely would result in my cancelling the set-up appointment I had just scheduled.

"Ok," she agreed, knowing it was easier for me to make decisions when I had clear facts to back them up.

I booked my first TMS appointment right after Christmas, so I decided to travel to Panama City Beach with Sarah and her family for the holidays. They rented a beach home with water views, white sands and magical sunsets, where I savored long walks along the Gulf of Mexico's shoreline, listening to "The Alchemist" and President Obama's autobiography, inspired by these hero journeys. We baked cookies to leave for Santa, hunted for seashells in the soft sand, watched the newly released Wonder Woman movie, and gazed at the Christmas Star alignment of Jupiter and Mars, where, for the first time in nearly 800 years, these planets came so close together, the naked eye could observe their celestial dance.

I yearned to endure the remainder of 2020 with the heart of a champion and the power of Wonder Woman. Yet, I was still anxious. Every day I fought the fear and uncertainty that welled up in my stomach as the TMS start date grew closer. No matter how many deep breaths I took, how many meditations I tried to focus on, or how many distractions I used to quell the unrest, it was still there. Perpetual. Unyielding. Growing louder, stronger, and more intense with each passing day.

Vacation's end came quickly and my sister's friends had graciously obliged me with a ride to the airport. I decided to fly back to Austin, departing a little earlier than the rest of the family, because I wanted to ensure I was fully prepared to start my TMS experience.

On the 20-minute drive from the beach to the airport, I quietly sat in the back of the car, consumed with the anxiety of the upcoming flight.

"*I've flown a million times,*" I told myself, knowing that number was clearly an exaggeration, but also knowing I had hundreds of thousands of lifetime sky miles under my belt. "*I'm in the plane,*" I said to myself as I visualized the next several hours, "*and everything's going well. The wheels touch down in Austin safely and you feel calm, and relaxed. You've got this.*"

To the rational, clear-headed me, this fear of flying made no sense. I'd been in planes since I was five years old and was a seasoned and competent solo traveler. Yet, I couldn't shake the negative belief that something bad was going to happen. It all was rooted in the panic attack I'd had on my way to San Diego four years prior. What I didn't yet realize was that it wasn't the flying that was keeping me stuck. It was what that panic attack actually meant, and all the loss that resulted because of my choices. In time, those losses would become some of my greatest gifts, providing purpose, clarity, and a larger life mission.

My sister's friends dropped me off at the departure area and, as I waited for the TSA agent to wave me up, I could feel the panic rising. It was an odd sense of floating and depersonalization, coupled with rapid-fire, irrational thoughts all conforming together to create tiny sparks of unhinged energy that pulsated through my body like a ping pong ball.

"*Oh fuck,*" I thought. "*It's happening. Shit. Shit. Shit.*"

Irrationally worrying that everyone around me knew what was happening, I started to imagine what it would look like if I came unglued in the TSA line. Utter embarrassment.

"*Pull it together,*" I scolded myself. "*Breathe. In one. Out three. In one. Out three.*"

It wasn't working. And the mask I was required to wear made breathwork even harder.

"Next," I heard the voice say, and looked up to see a female TSA agent waving me forward. I handed her my driver's license and placed my boarding pass against the scanner's red laser.

"Can you pull your mask down?" she asked me, eyeing my driver's license and then my face. She looked back down at the plastic card in her hand, and her demeanor changed. "Happy birthday!" she exclaimed, as I pulled the fabric back up over my nose and mouth.

"What?" I asked as she handed me back my identification.

"Happy birthday!" she said again, as if I should have known that I'd turned 46 a few days earlier. "We share the same one!"

Taking a pause to register what she was saying, my mouth finally caught up with my brain.

"Nothing like having a December birthday," I managed, and I wished her the same salutation as I shuffled over to the conveyer belt to complete the security screening.

After clearing security, it only took a few minutes to find the gate and, once I was there, I settled into a quiet spot, away from the tourists, to wait for the announcement to board. With the panic increasing, and the feeling of being completely disassociated and untethered from my earthly body, I decided to seek a lifeline. I dialed my sister's number with shaking hands. There was no answer. With a huge, anxious lump forming in my throat, I offered a quick prayer, pleading for calm, and then looked back at my phone. I wanted to call my sister's friend to ask her to turn around, come back to the airport where she had just dropped me off, and take me back to the beach cottage. The problem with that plan was that I didn't have her phone number. So, I was stuck.

I dialed my sister again and, this time she answered.

"I'm having a panic attack," I blurted out before she could even say hello. "The plane is about to board, and I don't think I can get on. I…I can't do this."

"Yes, you can," she assured me. "You do it all the time."

"Do you have any CBD?" she asked, signaling me to consider taking some of the non-THC elixir that was sloshing around in the little black bottle in my purse.

"Yes," I answered. "But I don't even know how much to take."

"Start with a dropperful," she suggested, "And see how you do. If that doesn't work, you can take another dropper. But give that first one a little time to kick in."

"You sure?" I asked.

"Yes," she assured me. "You'll be ok. I promise."

With that affirmation, I hung up the phone, took out the small bottle and opened the cap. Only a drop or two remained after I filled the glass dropper, so I went for broke and drank the remainder of what was in the bottle, including what I'd already piped out. Then I stood up and walked over to the newsstand that was directly across from the gate. I wanted to grab a paperback to keep my mind occupied on the plane ride back to Texas. By the time I finished the transaction and made it back to the boarding area, my entire boarding group was already on the plane.

"Last call for Boarding Group B," came the announcement. I knew it was now or never.

Stepping up to the gate agent, I scanned my ticket and walked down the gangway to the open door of the aircraft. As I got on the plane, my heart jumped and told me I needed to sit down. Immediately. People were putting bags into the overhead compartments, giving me time to scan the already filled rows and pinpoint the first available seat that would provide respite. The airline's open-seating policy made it a little hard to be selective but, at this point, I would have been ok with anything that would allow me to hunker down and let my brain relax.

On my left, in the first row, I saw my answer.

"Is someone sitting there?" I asked the young man, pointing over him and his dog, signaling to the open window seat.

"No. I'll move over," he said while simultaneously shifting himself, his things, and his dog towards the window.

"You don't have to do that," I countered. "I'm happy to take the window."

"Nah," he replied. "My dog is going to need the room."

I could tell he wasn't thrilled to be getting a seat mate, but I was too anxious to care much about anything except steel-knuckling through the plane ride without completely falling apart.

After sitting down in the aisle seat, I glanced over at his pup, a Boxer, wearing a black, military-style harness adorned with a smattering of patches. The pup was half the size of Meatball, and just as kind-faced and sweet as my own little guy.

I then looked back up at the man and quietly asked, "Army?"

"Yep," he answered.

"Well," I said, "thank you for your service."

I hated that phrase. It seemed so disingenuous when people said that to me, because I always wanted to ask them if they really understood the implications of what it meant to serve. But now was not the time to be ungracious, nor was it the time to have an internal philosophical debate about the words that just came out of my mouth.

"If that wasn't your service dog," I said to the veteran, "I'd give him all the pets in the world. He's the cutest."

The Boxer looked up at me, his big eyes begging me to follow through with that suggestion.

"Go ahead," the Army veteran said.

I put my unsteady hand in his bristly fur, slowly stroking the back of his neck, and then moving to pet the soft velvet of his ears.

They reminded me of Meatball's luxurious ears, which I routinely stroked when I felt nervous or unhinged. There was an air of familiarity of having a dog at my feet, providing the comfort I needed to reset my nervous system. His big Boxer eyes looked up at me with appreciation, and the three of us settled in for the long flight back home.

"I'm Kris," he said, extending his hand.

"Sue," I replied, meeting his with mine.

Once again, God had given me exactly what I needed in that moment, and more than what I needed for what was to follow. Kris and I became fast friends as his buddy, Chief the Boxer, settled in between us. We spent the plane ride swapping stories about being in the service and our experiences as veterans.

"You know," Kris said as we deplaned in Houston together, "I'm headed to Austin too. Maybe we should grab coffee or something while we wait?"

I looked at my watch, noting that we had a few hours until our next plane.

"Sure," I said, and we headed to a nearby coffee shop.

Sipping our drinks, we spent most of the layover talking about our aspirations and how we'd like to see life unfold.

"I want to open my own restaurant," Kris shared. "I have a space at a local church, cooking for them on occasion. And I do a lot of volunteering with *The Mission Continues*."

"No way!" I interrupted him, almost choking on my decaf vanilla latte as I lit up with excitement. "I was accepted into *TMC*'s Women Veteran's Leadership cohort!"

"Oh, that's a great program! You'll love it."

I was encouraged by his words, as I hadn't been sure what to expect when I applied. Their website had promised the opportunity to make lifelong friends and lasting connections, and I was excited at the prospect of bonding with women in the same ways I had at both guide school and during my Alaskan adventures.

"Our flight is about to board," I said a little while later. "We should head to the gate."

"Make sure you get on with me and Chief," Kris said. "We get to board first."

"You sure?"

"Absolutely."

We continued our conversation on the flight from Houston to Austin and, about an hour later, we were landing. We exchanged numbers and I was excited that I had pushed through excruciating fear and debilitating anxiety to gain a new friend and some key insights. I realized that, like Wonder Woman, I did embody the courage to face danger head-on. I was only here because I had listened to the glimmer to get on the plane, despite the anxiety and fear.

If I hadn't gotten on that plane, I would have missed out on meeting Kris and Chief and gaining confirmation that the Women Veteran's Leadership cohort was the next right step. I also realized that my worst anxiety, and panic, seem to happen right before something magical occurs. So, when future anxiety arose, I started asking myself, "*Is this something to be worried about, or is this here to signal the start of something epic?*"

Run Your Race, But Know Your Genetics

"Real change, enduring change, happens one step at a time."
– Ruth Bader Ginsburg

Right before heading to Florida, I elected to do pharmacogenetic testing, a DNA test which specifically would pinpoint how psychopharmaceuticals adversely or positively reacted with my genetic make-up. A week later, I received a 16-page, detailed report, as well as an invitation to meet with a provider to review the information. That conversation illuminated so many reasons why I had struggled for so long.

"Hi Sue, I'm Daniel," the provider said when I dialed into our scheduled phone conference. On this sunny December afternoon, I was much more interested in beach time and shopping than I was in digging into my mental health issues. I only had a few days left in Panama City Beach, but this was the only available time, so I knew I needed to make this meeting a priority.

"It looks like there's a lot to unpack," Daniel said. "Let's start with the SLC6A4."

"The what?" I asked him as I looked at the report and tried to make sense of the data points and colorful lines that were scattered across the multiple pages. I had tried all of the psych meds that were typically prescribed for depression and anxiety: Buspirone, Celexa, Clonazepam, Cymbalta, Effexor, Gabapentin, Lamotrigine, Lexapro, Paxil, Prozac, Trintellix, Valproate, Wellbutrin and Zoloft. Yet, nothing worked and most resulted in the side effects that they breeze over in the commercials - onset of brain fog, an increase in irrational feelings and emotions, uncontrollable mood swings, crying spells and increased thoughts of suicide. After the last go, Lexapro made me gain a lot of weight and still didn't manage the symptoms. I was at my wit's end with the constant yo-yoing and now, I felt like Daniel was about to explain the secrets that would unlock new possibilities.

"The SLC6A4," Daniel said, "is the serotonin transporter gene which determines how many Serotonin Uptake Inhibitors you have and how well they work."

I looked at the report in my hands, keying in on the row he was referencing. Glossing over the therapeutic implications, my eyes stopped at the large, yellow caution symbol in one column and, next to that, the note advising the importance of monitoring for adverse effects.

"There are two main ways this shows up in the body," he continued, "which include the long and the short variants. According to your report, you have the short variant, which means you have fewer Serotonin Uptake Inhibitors either present or working."

"What does that mean?" I asked.

"You don't respond well to the SSRI class of medications."

"Hmmm," I breathed into the phone, as I carefully tried to make sense of what he was saying. "So, that means most of the meds I've been prescribed the last 25 years were useless?"

Lightbulbs were going off at record speed. I thought about the psychiatrist who had once told me that prescribing psychiatric medication was not an "exact science" and all he could do was to move forward with his "best guesses" until he found something that worked. I thought about the countless doctors, and The Mayor, who didn't want to listen to me when I broached the subjects of hormones and genetics. I thought about all the times care teams decided it was easier to throw different medications at me instead of working through the complexity of getting to the root of the problem. My temperature rose, as I realized that even that small bit of information could have spared me years of heartache.

"Not useless. Just not the ones that would work the best with your genetic makeup," Daniel said. And then he shared another piece of critical information. "It looks like you also have high levels of dopamine in your frontal cortex, because your COMT gene doesn't break the dopamine down or get it to your liver for excretion."

"What does that mean?" I asked, now fully vested in this conversation. I was no longer worried about shopping or the beach. "I thought high dopamine levels were a good thing. Isn't that why we all doom scroll through social media? To get our next dopamine hit and feel better?"

This statement was tragically ironic, because the inauthenticity of social media never made me feel better.

"Well," Daniel continued, "excess dopamine can be associated with agitation, insomnia, high stress, anxiety and addictive behaviors."

"Wait – what?" I was stunned. He had just shined a light on a potential genetic link to my alcoholism and addictive tendencies. I used to joke that I just didn't have the "cut-off" switch like most people. Now genetics could be proving that my statement was, indeed, true? I was astonished.

As he went through the findings, I felt increasingly vindicated. I had erected mental roadblocks around using these drugs and internalized my own shortcomings for not being able to find one that worked. As side effects increased, or my tolerance decreased, I would complain and ask for different prescriptions. I would beg traditional doctors to help me find a reason behind the catastrophic failure of these SSRIs, SNRIs and mood stabilizers, and receive feedback that I was being irrational and ornery. I felt like I was the donkey they were trying to pin the tail onto, but they kept missing because the blindfold of misinformation had them all pointed in the wrong direction. And through this decades-long debacle, I ended up creating a very serious, and very real, traumatic response to psychiatric medications. Years later, I would try one more time to onboard liquid Lexapro, and the trauma response from even the smallest dose was so severe, I had to abort the attempt.

That is why I was starting to seek alternative options, looking into Hormone Replacement Therapy, meditative practices and TMS.

As we dug into additional data in my genetics report, the findings confirmed the things that had been floating around in my head for years. Much of what was showing up in this simple report helped me understand that my struggles were, in part, directly linked to my genetics.

"Also important to note," Daniel offered, "is that you carry the COMT Met/Met gene variation, which contributes to increased rumination. It can also make you more susceptible to depressive episodes."

I sat there reeling. For years, I couldn't understand why it seemed so much harder, if not nearly impossible, for me to change my thinking, or let things go, or react to stress in the same way that friends and family did.

"*Why can't I just look at all this stress, fear and anxiety as an opportunity to do something different? Why can't I just LET IT GO?*"

Like so many others, I had consumed libraries full of self-help books. I followed popular guidance which encouraged creating positive affirmations and visualizing different outcomes in an effort to decrease the negative thinking. Sometimes it was effective but, often it wasn't. I would shame-blame myself, thinking, "*What is wrong with me? I'm strong. I'm resilient. I'm educated. I should be able to handle this situation. I'm better than this.*"

But there is no "better" or "worse" because there is nothing you can do to change your genetic make-up. Our DNA is an unyielding expression that defines who we are and how our bodies react to life's tangible and intangible circumstances. Mental health disorders aren't discriminatory so, if our inherent DNA is a contributing factor to how we see, view and experience the world, the most we can do is become aware of our natural construct, accept the beauty in it, and establish our own best practices to mitigate our very unique blueprints.

"Here's my question," I asked Daniel, wanting an honest answer because I was awestruck at what we had just uncovered. "Why isn't this type of genetic testing standard protocol for all mental health practitioners?"

What we unearthed with a simple saliva swab answered questions that I had grappled with for years. I could have been on the path to healing with preciseness and more certainty decades earlier if only I had known about my genetic predispositions. For so long, I had been on that brutal assembly line, taking my meds, literally numbing the pain, and thinking I was doing the work to get better.

"I don't know," he said. And maybe he didn't.

My best guess was that it likely came down to cost and insurance. I'd paid for this test out-of-pocket, and it wasn't cheap. But there were some things that, to me, and to the efficacy of my healing journey, were worth the money. Information was one of these things and, on this warm December afternoon, in the middle of Panama City Beach, Florida, I finally found the treasure I had been seeking. I had found answers.

A River Runs Through Me

"Avoiding danger is no safer in the long run than outright exposure. The fearful are caught as often as the bold."
– Helen Keller

I showed up at the TMS clinic early on a Monday morning, with my fly fishing gear and a sack lunch left sitting in the back of my 4Runner. We had already done the initial session to gather the placement information, so it was time to settle into a regular routine.

When I entered the clinic, the young woman greeted me with a warm smile. I knew my way around, and made my way to the back room. With increasing trepidation, I slid into the TMS chair, and a flurry of activity quickly followed. As the back of my head found its place in the headpiece, the young tech secured the large magnet, verifying its placement using the imagery that glowed from the adjacent computer screen.

I had left my sister's house with the plan of heading to the Texas Hill Country directly following my first treatment. I wanted to spend the afternoon fly fishing and then make it back to Austin in time for an evening restorative yoga class. From my time in Montana, I knew I had the acumen to fish on my own. And, even though I didn't know the waters, I was ready to give it a shot. I was unfamiliar with which flies would work and how much tippet I needed for the bottom fly to swim along the water column in a realistic, and enticing way. It was intimidating to have to figure out an entirely new watershed on my own, but I was determined not to let that stop me.

Before coming to Austin, I made a Facebook post requesting guidance and suggestions for places to fish in the Hill Country. In another full-circle moment, a woman, whom I'd met a handful of years earlier when I was on a saltwater fly fishing adventure, alerted me to the fact that one of the fly fishing groups had opened their seasonal winter leases. With the beginning of a glimmer forming deep in my gut, I reached out to the group and asked if I could throw my name in the hat for consideration. These coveted private spots were known to go quickly, and I was under the assumption that they were hard to get because there were so few of them to be had. Within days, however, I was notified of my selection, and I received a season pass, which granted me access to an interconnected web of private lands and waters.

The Hill Country's fresh waters were an entirely different ballgame than my saltwater experiences, and freshwater fly fishing called for an entirely different playbook. I knew that I had four months to figure it out, and was grateful to have these lands and waters which would provide the lifeline I needed throughout my healing process.

"Ok," the TMS tech said, "we are all set."

She was ready, but I just couldn't get settled.

"Should we get started?"

"I…I just can't," I replied, in an angsty, guttural way. What had started as mild trepidation as I'd entered the building had turned into a full-blown panic attack.

"It's ok," she assured me, seeing fear in my eyes. "Why don't you take some time? We can either try again later today or start first thing tomorrow."

"Ok."

She unlatched the headpiece, and I stood back up out of the chair, looking for the quickest way to escape. Deep down, I knew that only way through this part of my healing journey was to literally sit in the mess. But I just wasn't ready.

I headed back outside, got into my 4Runner, and cried for an hour-and-a-half as I drove to the Hill Country. I needed the river to wash away my shame. I felt like such a failure, chastising myself for being a wimp. Forgetting about all of the insights I'd gleaned in Florida, and my propensity to not let things go, I leaned into the false narrative that everyone else would have been able to do this without issue. But here I was, breaking down, once again, which fed the lie that I needed to be stronger.

Arriving at the fishing lease, I parked in a small, deserted parking lot, pulled on my waders, strung up my 6-weight fly rod with a weighty olive Woolly Bugger, a good all-around fly that I taught my nephew to tie, and headed down to the river. As my feet met the coolness of the flowing water, I sent my first cast into the quiet and stillness of a Texas winter day. My fly landed with a thunk and I methodically started to pull the hefty bug back to the embankment, using a slow stripping motion that was meant to make the artificial fly move like a live baitfish.

Every few casts, I took a few steps to my left, moving purposefully upriver as I repositioned myself to fish the softer spaces, as well as the deeper pools. With so many varied features, including wild riffles and the long, unpredictable runs, this body of water was unique, dynamic and ever-changing. My mind started to slow down as I connected to the river, and the anxiety and panic from a few hours earlier slowly washed away with the downbound current.

After several unproductive casts, I finally decided it was time to tackle the "What do I do about TMS?" question. I'd come too far to bail on myself, but I was petrified to fully enter this new frontier.

"Ok God," I said out loud, where only the trees and birds could hear me. "If I land a fish on this cast, I'll go back this afternoon and start the treatment."

It was such a ridiculous conversation because, despite all the breadcrumbs and glimmers I had followed, despite the confirmation from the genetic testing and the research Sarah had done confirming mostly positive outcomes, I was still searching for a sign. I was still seeking clarity. I still wanted to have the 100% guarantee that TMS was the right thing for me. The problem is, in life there really are no guarantees. So, I just needed to be courageous enough to try.

I squared my stance, did a few false casts, not allowing my fly to touch the water, and then landed the Woolly Bugger in a spot about 45 feet upriver of where I stood. I started to pull the fly line back towards me with slow, gentle strips, matching the pretend baitfish's movement in the current of the river. As I pulled, I could see the line getting shorter, and my chances of finding an answer through that ridiculous bargain with God diminishing.

"Come on little guy," I said to the fish that I hoped was in nearby water. "Where are you?"

In that moment, with a resounding thud, my fly intersected with a fish's mouth and, as it took the Woolly Bugger, I realized, as I had many, many times before, that the Divine had me. I still had a defined role in my healing journey, but I was supported by a greater force than I would ever fully understand.

I landed a beautiful rainbow trout and, after removing the barbless hook and offering it a quick message of gratitude, released the fish back into the Texas current.

"*Here we go,*" I thought as I placed my rod and reel carefully in the bushes beside me so I could make the phone call and confirm my afternoon appointment.

When I made it back to the clinic, we repeated the process that now felt familiar. I sat in the big girl chair, with the magnet firmly in place, as the tech's finger hovered over the start button.

"You ready?" she asked.

"Yep," I said, this time with resolve, knowing that I wasn't alone.

The machine whirred to life. For the next 20 minutes, I could feel the PING, PING, PING on the front left side of my head and, despite wearing earbuds, which were piping in Oprah's voice as she read "The Path Made Clear," I could still hear every time the magnet reverberated against my skull. I was in the grind, and felt, in my core, that this is what resiliency looked like.

Over the next six weeks, I listened to audiobooks, podcasts and playlists, trying to transport myself inside of the story, the song, the conversation, and away from the unrelenting sound of the equipment. Sometimes I daydreamed, visualizing a future where I would write a book, or create retreats, or do something wildly impactful to help other women veterans. And, sometimes, my mind drifted back to more unsavory events, unexpectedly processing some of the things that had brought me here. As I closed my eyes one morning, my thoughts dipped back to my Coast Guard days, and a law enforcement patrol I had been on offshore of Central America. I was one of a few certified law enforcement officers on board our ship and had spent more than a month at

Coast Guard's Basic Boarding Officer Course, learning criminal law, defensive tactics, boating safety and conflict management. I had obtained the qualifications needed to board vessels at sea, search for illegal substances, migrants and other illicit happenings, and conduct maritime law enforcement operations. I graduated from the arduous Basic Boarding Officer Course as the Honor Graduate, which meant I was the top in my class after weeks of weapons training, role play scenarios, practice boardings, memorizing criminal law and statutes and acing a series of practical and written final exams. I came back to my unit fully qualified to lead at-sea law enforcement teams, yet the Cutter's captain never assigned me in that role. It didn't matter that I outranked my shipmates by grade. My male counterparts, who took lead on these boardings, outranked me by experience. So I was never the leader and only occasionally part of the team.

On this patrol, we had been tracking a fishing vessel in the Pacific Ocean that was suspected of drug activity. Early one morning, the captain decided it was time to get on board and confirm these suspicions. Temperatures were brutal as I donned my Kevlar body armor, full Operational Dress Uniform (ODU), steel-toed boots, and the law enforcement belt, which contained a pair of handcuffs, and empty spaces that, after visiting the ship's armory, would hold a baton, pepper spray, a 9mm SIG Sauer, and two extra magazines.

Once our four-person boarding team was ready, we launched our small boat into the choppy Pacific waters and made our way over to the fishing vessel. The Cutter remained within radio's distance, the other small boat at the ready in case anything went wrong. As we approached the boat, we were greeted by four dark-haired, scruffy men, who clearly had been at sea for a while.

Boarding the rickety boat using a Jacob's Ladder, our four-person team assembled on the bridge, where one of the men in question was bringing the fishing vessel to an idle speed. An intimidatingly large Coast Guard Boatswain's mate was in charge, and signaled to me, and one of the other team members, that we needed to stand watch over three of the boat's crewmembers while he, and one of the other boarding team members, took the captain to complete the paperwork and inspection.

"JG," the boarding officer said, referring to me by my Lieutenant Junior Grade rank instead of my name, "take watch."

"Gotcha," I replied as the other boarding team member and I took the three crew members and directed them to the nearest room, which was a small common area adjacent to the bridge. There was a bunk bed on the far wall, and a small bench nearer to where I stood. A window and the door formed a single point of entry, making it easier to keep an eye on things.

As we entered the room, two of the boat's crew walked over to the opposite wall and crawled onto the top bunk's droopy mattress. The remaining crewmember made himself comfortable on the bottom bunk. None of them seemed particularly disturbed by our presence as they sprawled out on the sagging beds, relatively non-plussed for having their entire morning upended.

My team member and I sat there for a while in silence, listening to the three men chatter incessantly. I stared at them, remaining stalwart, trying to pick up some of the Spanish dialect that ping-ponged from the top to the bottom bunk, and back up again. A mix of body odor that accumulated from days out at sea without a shower, and the remnants of dead maritime creatures that wafted up from the bowels of the fish holds, cataclysmically collided to create an obnoxiously pungent stench that filled the small room and made me want to vomit.

Apparently, I wasn't the only one.

"I need some air," my teammate said, as he stood up and walked towards the entrance, which also served as the exit. "I'll be right back."

Now standing the watch alone, I could feel the steady rocking of the boat as sweat beads accumulated beneath the t-shirt that was meant to be a barrier between my skin and the Kevlar vest. The stale air barely moved through our cramped space, and I willed myself to remain focused and engaged, in case anything arose that could lead to confirming the suspected illegal activity.

Unfortunately, the only thing that arose was a body part of one of the men on the top bunk, as he put his hand down his shorts and began to stroke himself. He wasn't blatantly exposed, and I didn't see any skin. They had taught us in boot camp never to abandon our post. So, I sat there, watching the firm and consistent movement of his arm – up and down, back and forth.

He was staring straight at me, a toothy grin emerging on his face.

"*Is he seriously…*" I thought to myself, unsure as to what action to take.

The other men were quiet, unmoving as I sat, locked in this uncomfortable power struggle with a grinning goon.

I wanted to use the tools in my toolbelt: pepper spray, handcuffs, a steel baton and a 9mm pistol, all at my fingertips. But I couldn't justify a reason to deploy any of them. The gun was out of play because, despite the man's lewdness, a lethal situation wasn't imminent, and the deadly force triangle wasn't complete. I didn't want to use my pepper spray in the stuffy room, as that wouldn't have turned out well for anyone, including myself. And I couldn't pull out my baton and beat him for beating off. Despite having a weapon for protection, training for awareness, and team members for support, I felt unsafe, alone and sickened.

I silently willed my teammate to hurry up. I didn't know where he had gone, or where we were at in the boarding process. And I didn't want to create an uproar by demanding that guy knock off his knocking off if there was no backup to quickly help me deescalate the situation. So, I sat quiet, stoic, watching him pleasure himself as he locked eyes with me.

"*Did I really give up my professional teaching career to be sitting here, in the middle of the ocean, watching some guy jack off?*" I wondered, internally in shock, as this was unfolding in real time.

"Time to go," the boarding officer's voice boomed from just beyond the room's doorway, and the grinning goon immediately ended his quest for pleasure.

I exited the stuffy room and sprinted over to the side of the boat, throwing my leg across the gunwale to get off the torture trawler as quickly as possible. With each foothold down the Jacob's ladder, I heard the yells of the toothy troll grow louder and louder.

"Ayyyyeee, linda!" came the vomit of words from his smirking pie hole. "Linda, linda, linda!" That word, repeated over and over, growing louder and louder as his smile became wider and more pronounced with each iteration.

I thought I was going to throw up, and not from sea sickness or the foul stench of the vessel. I knew he wasn't calling me *by* name but, instead, was calling me *a* name. "Beautiful, beautiful, beautiful," he kept repeating in Spanish as I departed. I didn't feel beautiful. I felt violated, disgusted and frustrated. And I felt alone. Getting back to the ship didn't provide the safety or comfort I needed because there was no one to talk to and no way to process this immense breach of my personal and professional boundaries. I was living on a floating boy's club, thousands of miles out to sea, trying to prove my grit, my worth, my tenacity. I already wasn't chosen as a primary boarding officer, despite my qualifications. So, how in the world was I supposed to go back to my commanding officer and let him know that I'd been deeply bothered by the man at sea who had choked his chicken while I had to sit by and watch?

I just imagined my experience becoming another joke that would circulate around the Cutter's small ecosystem. I had already been the target of ridicule when I reported gun shots from nearby pangas that turned out to be flying fish hitting the side of the ship's hull. Maybe not my best moment, but I was trying to lead through professionalism, and part of that meant standing a diligent watch. After that debacle, I wasn't interested in having a mockery made out of me, or this situation. So, I stayed silent.

I sat in the TMS chair, the relentless pinging of the magnet against my skull. I wanted to scream from the mountaintops that I deserved better. Every woman who had ever dealt with sexual abuse, sexual harassment and gaslighting deserved better. I deserved to feel safe, both in my job, and in speaking my truth. I deserved to not spend years convincing myself that this patriarchal behavior was normal, or that I should have been more demanding and made that man stop his stroke. I deserved the space and time to acknowledge that I had been hurt. And I deserved grace and compassion so I could heal.

But I didn't get any of these things. Instead, I got accolades for being assertive and admonishments when I wasn't. I got more gold stripes on my dress coat when I was accepted for promotion, visual cues, through the ribbons and medals that were pinned to the left side of my chest for a job well done, and constant non-verbal reminders that I needed to be hard, distant, angry and disconnected if I wanted to have a seat at the table.

The indoctrination to this way of thinking began in the chill of New Jersey's deep winter, with the banging of garbage can lids that served as our first bootcamp wake-up call. Over the next eight weeks, the creases in our hands would crack from throwing heaving lines in frigid November temperatures. Our individual voices would dim as we learned to speak as one unit – X-Ray 163. "Yes Sir! Yes Ma'am!" became the only appropriate answers and any questions I had about remaining a separate and distinct human slowly dissipated with each push-up, each scissor kick, each degrading comment that the Company Commander offered to the collective on our miserable performance.

Their job was to turn us from fledglings to fighters who could manage life in the fleet. And, at 27 years old, after two years in Africa, I wasn't quite prepared to give up that much of myself. But, as time went on, I convinced myself these processes were necessary to make sure we aligned, so we wouldn't hesitate in choosing Team over Self. I eventually believed that there was a method to the madness, ensuring we knew the processes and procedures which would keep us safe, help us look out for our Shipmates, and to work together as a team. And, for years, this belief system held me together.

That delicate thread was strong when it was enforced but could snap, and unravel the whole masterpiece, if it wasn't tended. So, the indoctrination continued well past bootcamp. Almost a year later, my dad traveled to New London, Connecticut, to pin on my

Ensign butter bars after I'd spent another 17 weeks at Officer Candidate School. And, once I was in the fleet, learning to lead in a way that was suitable for an organization that needed this type of structure to function, but not suitable to letting me live in alignment or authenticity, I slowly started to fray.

It was a slow burn, a progression that, over a decade, was successful at silencing my distinct voice. I spoke in approved messaging, acronyms and jargon. It was a series of methodical, calculated trainings that stripped away uniqueness and individualism, and replaced these things with conformity, with standards, with protocols that dictated so much more than hair color, nail length and clothing choices. In relegating myself to be known by my rank, or simply by the last name that was embroidered onto the name tape on my navy-blue cotton uniform, I became expendable. Replaceable. And utterly unremarkable. Because the system was never designed for me to be anything but these things.

As the TMS protocol continued, I thought back to my interactions with The Mayor, and realized our relationship stemmed from the same story being acted out, just with different characters and slightly different actions. By telling me I was making too much of a big deal out of something that he felt didn't need to be elevated, he was telling me my opinion and my boundaries didn't matter. But they did matter. And I mattered.

All of these instances stirred my Warrior Woman Spirit and when she showed up, she was pissed. Livid that I'd given into all of this bullshit for far too long. Angry that I had believed that I was just another cog in the wheel, disposable and dispensable, instead of the powerhouse badass that I now know myself to be.

"Be the starfish," she told me.

"What?" I asked her, a little surprised to feel the power of my own psyche show up so profoundly in this way.

"The starfish," she said again. "You are powerful. And capable. And worthy. Be the starfish."

"I'm trying," I pleaded. I had fought through so many obstacles and always found a way through. "What am I doing wrong?"

Exasperated, she simply said, "Be the motherfucking starfish, Sue."

And that was that.

"*Wow!*" I thought. "*My Warrior Woman is a little sassy…and a lot of badassy.*" I felt like the only appropriate answer to her direction was a clear, "*Yes ma'am*" and a lot more time figuring out what being a starfish really looked and felt like.

TMS didn't get easier, but the clinic agreed to let me bring Meatball to my daily sessions. We settled into a routine which included early morning treatments, followed by fly fishing in the Texas Hill Country, hiking in the nearby state parks, and ending each day with restorative yoga.

I think about that day on the river often and wonder what it would have looked like if I hadn't chosen to do the thing that was scariest of all. What if I hadn't taken decisive action or acted on my truth? What if I had listened to my false narratives, which would have had me move in fear, instead of hope? The choice to return to the TMS clinic, to embrace the unknown and trust that glimmer that told me this was the path forward, was one of thousands of choices I probably made that day. But it became a defining and important step on my healing journey.

Those days in Austin reminded me that I could, indeed, do hard things because I'd already done them.

My Mission Continued

"True self-care is not salt baths and chocolate cake. It is making the choice to build a life you don't need to regularly escape from."

– Brianna West

Around Valentine's Day, Austin's temperatures became unseasonably cold, bringing with them a historic ice storm that the city was not prepared for. Lasting a few days, unprecedented power and water losses ensued, keeping me hunkered down until I felt it was finally safe to brave heading back outdoors. Once the worst of it had passed, I resumed my daily afternoon walks, taking Meatball around a 4-mile loop in Sarah's neighborhood, and leaving Odin at home because the cold was too much for his frail and aging body. Bundled up in all of the winter gear I could find, including the Patagonia puffy jacket I'd packed at the last minute, we headed out to survey the aftermath. We were about 3 miles into our walk when my phone rang. Unsure if I wanted to remove my gloves to answer it, I glanced at the screen.

"*Where is '406'?*" I wondered, intrigued enough to uncover my freezing fingers so I could slide the answer button to the right and find out.

"Hey Sue," the male voice said through the headset, "I'm calling from USDA Rural Development, in Bozeman, Montana."

I was rolling though my internal rolodex, trying to figure out why USDA was calling me.

"Listen. I know you applied for the Public Affairs position a while ago. I'm just calling to see if you are still interested."

Meatball and I stopped walking, and I took in the tiny icicles that dotted the Live Oak trees along the boulevard. These small crystals looked like flower buds, each perfectly formed, attached formidably to the branches.

He was waiting for my response, as I thought about the glimmers I had followed, much like these tiny ice formations that were sparkling with diamond-like brilliance in Austin's late afternoon sun. Listening to the glimmer which nudged me to take a four-month sabbatical over a thousand miles from home had been hard enough. I'd been worried about taking that much time off work because, without a paycheck, I didn't know how I would make my mortgage. Yet, over the course of that period, God showed up in big and small ways. My *Project Healing Waters* fly fishing group from Charleston sent fly tying materials to keep me occupied. Karen sent a t-shirt reading, "My dog thinks I'm great" (which, when I looked in the mirror reflected back as "My God thinks I'm great"). My teammates, whom I thought I had abandoned, called almost daily to check on me, and people working for the federal government, some of whom I hadn't talked to in years, donated exactly enough leave time to provide me with income for the duration of my sabbatical. So, as I considered if I was ready to entertain the idea of moving my life to Montana, to a mountain town I knew little about, something told me things would somehow come together if that was where I was meant to go.

"Yes, I'm still interested."

"Fantastic!" he said, sounding relieved that we were moving forward with the next steps.

I closed out the conversation with a date and time for the interview and lingered for a moment to take in the icy beauty around me. Everything was still. Quiet. I was rooted in this moment, in this space, where I knew, to my core, that everything was going to be ok.

It had been at least a month since I had submitted that application. I didn't have any family or close ties to Montana – just a few gals whom I'd met during guide school and regularly kept in touch with. I had visited Bozeman decades earlier, when I was married to my first husband and his daughter lived there. But a lot of water had passed under my proverbial bridge since that time, so my only Bozeman references were a few college road trips, the time in guide school, and the week-long fly fishing trip on the Bighorn. I knew nothing about Montana's sub-zero winters, what it meant to live and work in a rural community, or what it would feel like to live in nature's playground, complete with mountains, rivers and valleys to explore.

As I anxiously awaited interview day, I focused on the Women Veterans Leadership Program, which was stretching and strengthening my confidence, lifting my voice, and helping me understand how to become a different kind of leader. In the culminating assignment, we were asked to craft a personal narrative, with a call to action, that would be shared with the cohort.

"I'm a woman, a veteran, a professional, a daughter, a sister, an aunt, a fly fisherwoman, a seeker, a wanderer, a volunteer, a Christian, a yogi, a visionary, a leader, a dog-lover, a patriot, a world-traveler, an adventurer, a giver, a writer, a boat captain, a

gardener, a motivator, a warrior, a fighter. These are all elements of myself that make me uniquely me." I wrote. *"As a strong woman, I was too afraid to publicly admit my suffering because I didn't want anyone to know I was slowly becoming unhinged. So, I maintained my desperate façade of appearing 'normal,' as any well-established leader would. Personal experience has taught me that, without taking the time to understand the root causes for our discontent, and without doing the hard and tedious work of unravelling from these root causes, we don't actually fix anything. If this journey has taught me anything, it's that we must embrace the suck by owning our pain and sitting through the suffering so we can become fully equipped to lead a Big Life."*

As my call to action, I noted that I would be launching a podcast to help female veterans build authentic, empowered communities. But it would take more healing, and two-and-a-half additional years before I actually hit publish on the first *Two Gals and a Mic* episode. And, when I did, Carolina, a Navy veteran, entrepreneur and self-made fashion designer, whom I'd met in this program, was my first guest.

When I heard Carolina's personal narrative, I knew that she was exactly the right person to kick things off. She said, "I think we all have a talent, skill or ability that is so unique to each and every one of us. So, my call to action is to really invite everyone to bring that out of themselves and share it with someone else. Even if you think that what you do is not that amazing, or even if you're doing something that you don't think is that great, it might be appreciated by someone else if you have the courage to start sharing."

Sharing stories became a core element of my personal mission and, five years after meeting Carolina, I wrote an updated version of my own personal mission statement.

"I am a powerful Woman Warrior. I have walked through the fire to reconnect with my authentic self, to use my voice, and create ways through story, fly fishing and nature-based experiences to help other women do the same."

That statement became my purpose. My why. And my North Star.

My interview with USDA went well, and I accepted the position in Bozeman. Then I turned my energy and attention to tackling the new challenges of locating a place to live, setting up movers, and planning my South Carolina exit strategy. My anxiety skyrocketed, and I'd like to say that the next steps were easy. But they weren't.

As I sat at Sarah's dining room table, I was deliberating my start date and felt unnerved by the enormity of everything that needed to get done to make the move out West.

"Sue," she said, "there are plenty of ways to tackle this. Just take a minute, figure out your next best step, and then do something about that one next step. You don't have to have everything figured out at once."

Taking things one step at a time was never a strong suit of mine. But I heeded her advice and leaned into approaching this enormous change through a calculated and pragmatic approach. I extended my reporting date for my new position so I would have time to book a moving company and pack my house. Then I called my realtor and put my beachy cottage up for sale. As soon as that happened, one of the gals from fly fishing guide school connected me with a real estate agent in Bozeman and I found a place to rent in a market where rental properties were scarce.

And, in a low point that came in early spring, just before I had to briefly return to South Carolina to finalize all the details, I took Odin for one last spin in the steadfast red wagon so he could see his favorite places one last time. My heart ached as we said our final goodbyes later that afternoon, but he was ready to go run with Harlie over the Rainbow Bridge.

Even though things seemed muddled, the pieces were coming together. It was still foggy, but I knew that the fog couldn't stay forever. At some point, the sun had to come out.

The Road Not Taken

"Two roads diverged in a yellow wood,
And sorry I could not travel both...
I took the one less traveled by,
And that has made all the difference."
– Robert Frost

Moving to the mountains wasn't something I'd seriously considered ever doing again, since leaving Denver in my early 20's. Following commencement from the University of Denver, I'd moved away and, aside from a couple of years in Southern Ethiopia, I made deliberate choices to live by the beach, or within close proximity of the ocean. Beach, sand, boats – these were the things that brought me comfort. And, deep down, I was worried that the rugged, wild, mountainous landscapes of the West would remind me too much of a childhood I didn't want to relive.

If I'd listened to my head, instead of my intuition, I never would have had the courage to explore the glimmers which would put me on the exact right path. If I only sought out the sure things, or the things that didn't require an extraordinary amount of faith in lieu of fear, I never would have considered moving to Montana. Instead, I likely would have stayed in South Carolina, seeking a more reasonable choice that would not have required moving across the country solo.

But, in that stagnation, I also would have sacrificed growth and not gifted myself the self-awareness that came with reestablishing my life in a place where the possibilities were endless. The strength that resulted from forging community, roots, rhythms and patterns, when the only thing that was certain was an untamed frontier, felt a little reckless, wild and overtly freeing. As I look back, I am confident that if I had not chosen the road less taken, I would have dimmed my light and extinguished the hope that was starting to glow in my soul.

That's the funny thing about the way life unfolds. Circumstances happen that catapult us into the unexpected and we can choose to wither or bloom. Blooming takes courage because the process of being planted, watered and brought to the flowering stage can involve a whole lot of pruning and growing pains. Yet, it's exactly the things that we don't want to have to suffer through which give us perspective. And beauty often comes from the darkest of places.

So, on a May morning in 2021, without much fanfare, I packed up my 4Runner for a second time and, with Meatball as my steadfast companion, headed West for the adventure of a lifetime.

I spent five days on the road, sleeping in my truck and visiting state parks along a route that was as multifaceted as it was geographically diverse. Meatball and I camped our way across the northern part of the United States, taking short diversions along back roads and less-traveled pathways. We stopped to explore gravel and dirt trails, to wet the line and hunt for fish, and to stand in awe of larger-than-life sculptures which dotted North Dakota's barren landscape. We dipped into coffee shops well off the beaten path, where the aroma of Grandma's cinnamon apple pie swirled in my nostrils as I ordered just a sandwich. To go. And, on the last night, we stayed in a tiny campground where bison ambled freely, blocking our ability to do the same.

We landed in the Big Sky state on May 11, and, as Meatball and I crossed Montana's state line, I stopped briefly to take a quick video at the Montana state sign. Despite the snow that was falling, I stood by the side of the highway, in socks and flip flops, and cried. These were tears of joy. Tears that showed my perseverance and grit and determined stamina which propelled me through the hardships to get to a place where I trusted I would be able to grow and thrive. I was proud of myself for choosing to listen to that small feeling in my gut, the intuitive love language that called me to follow a different path – albeit one that seemed crazy and uncertain from the onset. The only known quantities were a job and a place to live. Yet, somehow, I believed everything would eventually settle down and, as I created a new life, I would find the healthy and healing rhythms that would allow me to cultivate community and start to thrive.

As I settled into my new job with USDA, I could feel the uncertainty and unpredictability from the past several months dissipate, replaced by assuredness and more hope. My corner office had windows that lined the wall beside my desk, with an unimpeded view of the Bridger Mountains peeking out from the other side of the glass. The snowcapped peaks were slowly giving way to the green lushness that Montana's springtime brings, and I could feel the heaviness that had lived in my heart for years, starting to break free.

The office was quiet and, with COVID protocols still in place, Meatball and I were often the only occupants of the beautifully crafted building. The cubicles and offices that once had been brimming with employees were empty. But I didn't mind. In fact, I loved coming into my quiet corner every day, without the distractions of small talk and drive-by taskings. The peace and tranquility of that space allowed possibility to fill my computer screen as I created short videos, stories and strategic communication strategies to elevate the successes of farmers, ranchers, entrepreneurs, homeowners and municipalities around the state. Meatball and I would take mid-morning breaks, walking around the block, breathing in the mountain air and bathing ourselves in the warmth that settles in when wildflowers are peeking through the last remnants of snow, and bees, butterflies and hummingbirds are playfully foraging amongst the budding blossoms.

After one of those mid-morning breaks, I sat back down at my computer, feeling connected, purposeful, and excited about a video I was working on. With my back to the office's door, a dulcet female voice brought me back into the room.

"Good morning, Sue," the voice said. "I'm Donna."

I turned my chair around to face a middle-aged woman, and was immediately struck by her powerful stance, offset by a warm, welcoming energy and beaming smile. She reminded me a little of Karen.

"I work over in Community Development."

"It's really nice to meet you!" I was genuinely excited to meet new people, and promised myself, on the drive across the country, that I would make a concerted effort to find my community.

"Oh!" she squealed before I could add anything more to my greeting. "Who's this?" her voice relaying an obvious love for the babies with fur and four legs.

Meatball's nose collided with her outstretched hand, and his body leaned into hers, already searching for the behind-the-ear scratches and pets.

"Sorry," I said, moving quickly to remove his Velcroed body from hers. "This incorrigible guy is Meatball." I worried that his presence at the office was going to now create problems because, technically, he wasn't supposed to be there.

"Oh, it's ok," Donna replied. "I have a Golden Retriever named Harper. And she's the same way."

I smiled, relaxing a little bit as I grabbed Meatballs's collar and moved him back to his spot behind my desk.

"We should take them hiking sometime," Donna offered. "Do you like to hike?"

"I love to hike!"

"Yeah, me too," she said. "I hiked a lot when I was in Alaska."

"You lived in Alaska?" I asked. I was intrigued by her backstory.

"Yeah. I was in the Air Force," Donna offered. "I was living up there for a while, with my daughter, before I came to Montana."

"I was in the Coast Guard!" I was so excited to not only meet another woman veteran, but one who was strong, gracious and loved dogs.

We spent the next several minutes talking about wild places and spaces, recognizing that we had a lot in common, and leaving room and curiosity for the things that were yet to be discovered. In that initial encounter with Donna, I felt connected, rooted, seen and heard. Her kind words and interest in getting to know me affirmed that God had put me in exactly the right place, at exactly the right time. Even though I was still trying to find my footing in navigating a whole new landscape, I knew, beyond a shadow of a doubt, that we were going to be fast friends.

Donna and I spent the summer exploring different trails with our pups, and they too grew to be buddies. As we put miles on the dirt paths, we shared our struggles, our stories and our successes. We shared our fears, and our hopes for the future. I let myself test the waters of authenticity, each conversation going a little deeper, with a little more honesty, and slowly bridging the gap between feeling like I had to do it all by myself and knowing that I had people to walk the path with. I could be raw. I could be real. I could be me. And Donna never flinched. She encouraged. She walked alongside. And she lit a fire under me to do the things I never thought were possible. Now, half a decade later, Donna and I have forged an iron friendship, sharpened by the challenges that life continues to throw at us.

In fact, Donna was my second *Two Gals and a Mic* podcast guest, sharing her powerful insights into doing what it takes to achieve big goals.

"I just decided to sign up for a Spartan class because I work from home now and I want to be around people," she shared in our interview. "And they were like, come on, Donna, let's do a Spartan race. And so, I did."

As a powerlifting champion, I knew Donna was fierce. But her willingness to put herself out there, and try something new at 60 years old, was next level.

"How did you get through all of those obstacles?" I asked her as we chatted about the experience.

"Honestly, I was really scared to do it. You don't really know what to expect. It was in the mountains of Montana, and it had rained and been cold all weekend. But I had a really good coach who said, 'Donna, I'm doing this with you every step of the way.' And just having that person there, to support you and encourage you, meant the difference between success and failure."

"Is that not a metaphor for life?" I asked.

"Right?" she agreed. "There were 23 obstacles. I had to crawl on my belly, under barbed wire, and I had to climb over a four-foot wall, a six-foot wall, and an eight-foot wall. I had to climb 250 feet up a cargo net, up over the top and down the other side. I had to pick up a 75-pound round concrete ball and walk, I don't know, 50 yards with it. And remember, it had been raining, and everything's muddy, and I'm picking this up out of the mud and trying to carry it without dropping it because if I dropped it, I would have had to do 30 burpees. And I did not want to do burpees, so I held onto that thing for dear life."

"I know that when I crossed the finish line during my Ironman, there was this immense sense of wonder and awe," I reflected. "And I realized it was not necessarily about crossing the finish line, but more about what I learned through the course of the journey. What did Spartan teach you?"

"I learned I'm a lot stronger than I thought I was, and I'm capable of a lot more than I thought I was," said Donna. "And that felt really good to know."

A few years after that conversation, I would join Donna on the Spartan course, for my first Spartan race, and her third. On that rainy June morning, Donna was with me every step of the way. We navigated seemingly insurmountable climbs over slippery walls, bear crawls under barbed wire fences, farmer carries with buckets full of rocks, and traversing cargo nets up and down steel A-frames.

Every obstacle was another opportunity to test our strength, our fortitude, and our willingness to get dirty as we cheered each other on. As Donna and I clasped hands and jumped over the fiery finish line, I knew that I'd just completed something that, a year before, I wasn't able to master. I didn't get there because I had gained physical strength in the 12 months since my previous attempt. It wasn't because I'd spent months training, as I had with the Ironman. It wasn't because my broken back felt any less pain. I crossed the Spartan finish line because I'd found my Tribe. That group of people cheered me on, supporting me through each and every obstacle, with the firm belief that, even in my imperfection, success was possible.

Success had been a long, hard road, and only of late had been filled with a little more risk and a lot more alignment. In early February 2022, I was invited to speak at a conference to talk about the healing qualities that nature provides. My focus was on creating space and a place for women veterans in the outdoors. I wanted to share some of my own experiences and the importance of integrating nature with the healing process. So, I showed up, laptop in hand, and walked a small group through my PowerPoint presentation at one of the breakout sessions. While it wasn't a landmark attendance, I realized later that my involvement at that conference wasn't about my presentation. Or getting more women playing in the outdoors. Instead, my critical takeaway would become the nuggets of wisdom everyone else gifted. As I attended sessions, talked to people, and listened, my internal spark became a blaze, and then a full-blown wildfire. That conference on Outdoor Leadership helped me understand that I was being called to create movement, space and opportunities for women to heal. I was on the right path, and that path was leading to formidable destinations that I could not yet even imagine.

Before leaving for the conference, I repurposed a small business I'd started when I was in Charleston, and launched *Two Gals and a Boat, LLC* as a women's fly fishing education course, driven to create safe, outdoor spaces for women to be in community, on the water, creating success in areas that caused them uncertainty.

As I'd experienced in guide school, there was power in learning together, so I created a curriculum to offer a series of carefully curated fly fishing classes, for women, by women. I wanted to offer small, personalized classes that built a strong foundation, so women felt confident to explore the outdoors on their own or with others. Each class built on the foundational pieces from the sessions before, as I incrementally introduced the basic skills needed for them to feel comfortable on the water and in the wild. My vision was to create space for women to make connections while learning fly fishing and conservation principles.

The website had been live for a short period of time when I had the opportunity to take a local news reporter and get him out to the river to do a pre-recorded piece on *Two Gals and a Boat*.

"Hey Donna," I said, as she answered her phone a few days before the interview, "I'm meeting with a reporter from the local CBS affiliate to talk about *Two Gals*. Do you want to do this with me?"

"Sue," she replied, "I don't know anything about interviews."

"Come on," I pleaded. "It'll be fun. I promise." And it was.

It was an early March morning; the temperatures still cool enough to warrant a hat and puffy jacket. The warmth of our collective breath created vaporous clouds that dissipated just as quickly as they appeared as Donna and I stood in the parking lot unpacking our gear.

We chose to meet the reporter by a section of the Gallatin River that meandered through a more urban part of the Gallatin Gateway community, because it was convenient, quiet, and accessible. I had first met the reporter when he covered a story I had pitched for work. So, when I sent this idea his way, he was excited to come out to the river and experience an entirely different side of me.

"I think this is really cool," he said, gathering his camera, lavalier, and tripod as the early morning chill caught us all a little off-guard. "I love the idea of bringing more women to this space. But," he said, looking directly at me, "I want to know your why. Why fly fishing?"

I had done enough interviews and press conferences to know that even though the camera wasn't rolling, everything was on the record. This needed to hit.

"When you empower a woman to do great things, maybe in a space where she has uncertainty and fear, you've just opened up a world of opportunity," I said. "She will take those skills and translate them to other areas of life. And that is where ideas become actions."

And there it was. I had just declared, to the reporter, to Donna, to the world, that this new idea of mine was no longer just an idea. My Thought Leadership was no longer Thought. In that moment, it had transformed to Leadership in Action.

The interview ran on the evening news and was posted to the station's website. With that infusion of publicity, it didn't take long for my phone to ring. As I sat on my living room couch, watching Netflix and basking in the afterglow of the segment which had aired a few hours earlier, my caller ID illuminated with the words "Unknown Caller." A small, excited lump settled in my throat, as I quickly prepared my talking points and readied myself to answer questions about the *Two Gals* program. This was the second time my phone had rang since the news story aired, and there was still something so surreal about watching my dream taking shape.

"Hello?" I answered, my excitement building.

"Is this *Two Gals and a Boat*?" the female voice asked.

"It is!" I could have leaped out of my chair, wanting to hug the caller on the other end of the line because she cared enough to reach out, to find out more about how we would, together, build community, connection and conservation. I was ready to answer her questions about my classes and share my vision and my dream.

However, instead of curiosity and interest, I was met with contempt and negativity by a random person who wanted to push me down before I even had a chance to stand up.

"We have enough people on our rivers, you stupid c---" I couldn't believe what I was hearing. And then the line went dead.

I sat there, staring at my phone, as if it would give me answers as to why a total stranger felt she had the right to come at me, albeit anonymously, to try and steal my joy and my power.

As I tried to shake it off, the doubt crept in. The same, worn internal dialogue that told me that I wasn't good enough, that I didn't know enough, that I needed to just step down.

What God would tell me, that the caller did not, was that I was made for this. The Divine put this song on my heart and gave me everything I needed to make it a reality. All I needed to do was get out of my own way.

So, I stepped aside from the doubt and fear and, in their places, filled those voids with actionable items that created tangible results. I sold all the available seats for the 2022 cohort, as well as the 2023, 2024, and 2025 seasons. I learned about fisheries conservation, even transitioning my professional work to the U.S. Fish and Wildlife Service. I honed my fly fishing skills, spent more time in the drift boat, and created the community, connection and conservation that I had advertised as my mission areas.

But, despite these advancements, I was still holding myself back from fully embracing my Warrior Woman spirit and being the starfish. I reflected on the progress I had made with TMS, realizing that the work I'd done to resolve the major depression was remarkable. However, if I was going to turn my mission into a movement, it would require my willingness to address my PTSD. It was time to step out of the Post Traumatic Stress Disorder and into Post Traumatic Growth.

Turning Struggle Into Strength

"The cave you fear to enter holds the treasures you seek."
– Joseph Campbell

My counselor had mentioned Post Traumatic Growth (PTG) as a way to work through my PTSD, so I spent some time researching the science before searching for a way to apply these principles in my own life. I knew I wouldn't be able to do that without some concrete guidance, and stumbled upon the *Boulder Crest Foundation*, which offered a week-long Warrior Progressive and Alternative Training for Helping Heroes (PATHH) retreat. Based on the science of PTG, the website promised to "transform your struggle into strength and thrive in the aftermath of trauma." I was intrigued, so I applied.

The screening process was stringent. After the initial online application, I had a personal interview with the team leader to determine if I was a good fit. We chatted about my desired outcomes, and he offered some insight into the program, but not as much as I was hoping for.

Just as I had sought the Plan of the Day when I was in the hospital, I wanted to understand the play-by-play for this week-long training. I was accustomed to receiving an itinerary in advance of any program I attended. In the past, with this information, I could apply my own lens and my own judgments to the coursework that would follow.

However, in this case, there wasn't a lot of information. No itinerary sent in advance. No outline of what to expect. Just a packing list, an airplane ticket, and details on where to meet at the airport once I arrived.

I hated not knowing who I was meeting or what the specifics of the week would look like. Operating in the gray had never been one of my strong suits, and Warrior PATHH took that to a whole new level. But, as I would come to understand, nothing was without purpose. This was just the tip of the iceberg of an intricate puzzle that would come together to form a clear and distinct picture of what healing and thriving could look like. Putting the puzzle pieces together would take time, and, I would pick them up, one by one, as I went through the weeklong retreat, the 90 days of post-retreat study, and the multiple years of connection and support that I would continue to lean into from the other retreat participants, who, like me, were finding their ways as we struggled well together.

The mid-afternoon October sun blazed across the runway as my plane touched down in Atlanta. I watched the fumes from the mixture of jet fuel and heat bounce off the runway as we made the long taxi to the gate. I wasn't sure what was in store for the week ahead, but I hoped that, whatever "it" was, it would be transformative. I'd set my bar high, wanting to experience the same success as I had with TMS. I hadn't been back to Atlanta since I'd picked up Odin from the adoption agency three years prior. Walks on the beach with his little red wagon seemed like eons ago, and I marveled at the complex passage of time as the aircraft slid into the gate.

"Ding. Ding. Ding," the overhead bell beeped, signaling it was safe to remove our seatbelts, stand up and get ready to deplane. Air travel had gotten easier, and I had set up a calming ritual that helped me navigate through it with much less anxiety. As I stood in the aisle, waiting for the first-class passengers to grab their items and make their way out of the plane's front door, I pulled out my phone and reread the meeting instructions.

"Once you arrive in Atlanta, you will head to baggage claim and gather your belongings. A guide from your program will reach out to you that day to coordinate an exact location to meet up. If anything should happen on your day of travel, such as a delay or missed connection, please let us know as soon as possible so we can ensure you have been accommodated accordingly."

"*That's weird,*" I thought as I scrolled through my text messages and checked my voicemail. I didn't see any additional messages or missed calls from anyone, so I wasn't sure what they meant by, 'someone would reach out.'

I headed to baggage claim. The airport was packed with travelers moving in all different directions, and I played Frogger through the terminal as I made my way to the other side of Security and down to the main floor. Dodging the crowds, I could feel that unwelcomed prickly feeling of anxiety churning in my stomach. It was a demanding mistress and today, I just didn't have the time, or desire, to give it any attention. So, to combat its progression, I breathed in deeply, put my head down, and walked faster.

It took me no time to arrive at the baggage claim area, where I saw my gray bag circulating on the metal belt. With a forceful tug, I pulled it towards me, tipped it upright on all four wheels, and then moved to a spot nearby to wait.

The minutes ticked by, and my eyes moved between checking my phone to see if that "someone" had reached out and scanning the area to see if that "someone" would just appear.

After ten or so minutes, a young woman cajoled her large bag off a nearby carousel and then made her way over to where I was standing. I gave her a quick smile, and then turned my attention back to my phone, hoping to see the text message that would indicate where we were supposed to meet. I noticed she was checking her phone earnestly, and I began to wonder if we were waiting for the exact same someone. But I never bothered to ask, thinking it would be weird and awkward to strike up a random conversation with an airport stranger about a Post Traumatic Growth retreat, especially if that wasn't why she was there. So, I kept my mouth shut, as we both stood in silence, scrolling through our phones and staying locked and isolated in our tiny little worlds.

Twenty minutes later, a tall man with a cowboy hat and a smile that could light up the night sky, like stars dripping from an onyx canvas, bounded towards the two of us. As he came into view, I could see he was wearing a *Boulder Crest* logoed shirt and a name badge that made him look even more official.

"Hey there," he said, with a slight twang as he pushed his outstretched hand towards me. Entering my bubble with a few more steps, he followed up his greeting with a question. "Are you with PATHH?"

"Yes," I replied, offering my hand in return, and wondering how he knew to approach me. But then I noticed that my silent friend offered her hand as well, and I surmised that maybe he was in search of two missing women, with big suitcases, which would round out the crew of seven he had been sent to pick up.

"Great!" he said, corralling the two of us. "The rest of the group is over here. We need to get going pretty soon, so if you need anything before we head out, you'll want to make it quick."

I turned to my new friend, offered another smile, and this time a proper greeting.

"Hi," I said to her, "I'm Sue."

"Shannon," she said as she returned my smile.

I knew immediately I was going to like her. There was something warm and inviting in the way she held herself, and I regretted not saying anything earlier. How many wasted minutes went by as we stared into our phones because society had convinced us that random conversations with strangers were dangerous? And weird? As a child, I was taught to never talk to strangers. That makes sense when you're five but maybe should be given a little more consideration when you're almost ten times that age.

We gathered our belongings and made our way over to the gaggle of women and their comparably large suitcases as we waited for further instructions. We were led out to the parking lot, and to the two large SUVs which were waiting to take us to Camp Grace, about an hour-and-a-half drive from the airport, in the little town of Roberta.

Once we made it to camp, and settled into our rooms, we convened for lunch and it didn't take long for the seven of us to get past the pleasantries and into the heart of what sisterhood felt like.

For years, my head and my heart felt disconnected, and this incongruence stole the hope, the joy, the spark from my spirit and stunted my ability to thrive. But, in this short week, with this group of highly trained, dedicated and kindhearted souls, the connective tissue began to regenerate – just like the starfish, regrowing the appendages that had been lost in battle.

In one of our first exercises, our PATHH guides encouraged us to write down our goal for the week. What I penned became a larger aspiration of the way I wanted to continue my journey.

"To be authentic," I wrote, "and live in integrity so I can continue to say 'yes' to the next right thing which aligns with my soul's purpose."

It would take less than a day to realize that the other women, who hailed from towns from across the nation, would not only help me live into that ethos while I was in Georgia but would continue to light my path long after those Southern lights had dimmed.

We all came from different backgrounds and had different experiences. Some in the group had been first responders, some had served in the military, some had been nurses during COVID, and some had been on the frontlines in 9-1-1 call centers, responding to the absolute worst scenarios that humankind had to offer.

"I had a horrible personal tragedy, while I was at work," Erin told us, and then later shared on the podcast. "I was sitting conversing with one of my co-workers, and a call popped up on the screen for dispatch." Erin had been a 9-1-1 operator, in the dispatch center, and came from a long line of first responders. "The co-worker that I had just been visiting with looked at me, and her face just went sheet white. I turned and looked at the screen and it was my sister-in-law's address. I immediately picked up the line and said, 'What's going on?' It was my 10-year-old nephew who said, 'Krista fell in the pond and Mom's doing CPR on her.' At the time, that was my 18-month-old daughter. To make a long story short, she did not survive."

My heart broke the first time Erin shared this story, again when she retold it on the podcast, and a third time when I edited the episode. But, in that tragedy, Erin found purpose and now works with veterans, military members and first responders to find ways to help them through their struggles. "What really ended up allowing a shift for me," she would later share, "was being vulnerable and open enough with other people, and really connecting, which is something I had avoided for so long because I felt so broken and so damaged."

The more we allowed each other into our hidden stories, the more we collectively healed. But we did it together. And, once again, I recognized the power of the collective story.

Carrie, a firefighter turned paramedic, told a story that resonated with me deeply. As she spoke of taking on the *Good Old Boys Club*, I could feel my frustration rising because I didn't want other women to have this be their lived experience too.

"I faced a lot of 'you can't do this,' 'you won't be able to,' 'you're not strong enough,' 'girls are too emotional,' all of those things that we all hear," she told us candidly. "And then you try to swing the other way with too much of 'I won't show any emotion,' and 'I'm going to be super tough.' Well, that doesn't work for us either. It's not what we are. We are women."

And, as a yoga instructor who taught mindfulness and meditation at the fire houses, Carrie did a beautiful job of reminding us that it's not selfish to practice self-care.

"I try to schedule in times," she offered. "I think it's important to prioritize those things and let the people around you know that it's a priority. It's important to keep up your self-care routines, that you make yourself a priority, because you can't pour from an empty cup. So, you have to fill yourself up in order to give to others."

As we shared our goals, and the reasons why being at PATHH, and being with each other, were important, it became evident that we were more similar than we were disparate.

"How do you move, with these memories and scars," we pondered, as we penned a song together at the end of the week, "fighting through the fear to get to here, right where we are? How many hands did it take to hold us up, finally found our Tribe and learned to just embrace the suck. No backing down…we're buckin' up."

That's how we began the journey that we are still on together. There was no backing down from the hard stuff – just a shared understanding that, despite the rawness of the stories we shared, the battles we fought, and the circumstances we overcame, our group was fierce. We were so much more than survivors. We were Fighters. Victors. Champions. A group of Bold Women Warriors. I had found my Tribe, and in this space, I had connected with amazing women, a group of Beautiful Badasses, who quickly became my Sisters.

As the week unfolded, things that had been stuck for years surfaced, and the lightbulbs turned on, one after another, illuminating the parts of my soul that had been dormant and abandoned for decades. This shift created an expansiveness that would allow me to hold space for my Sisters as we navigated the transformation together.

"Be where your feet are planted," our PATHH Guides would constantly remind us. "When you spend too much time in the past, you dwell on sadness and loss. When you focus too much in the future, you get lost in fear and anticipation. But, staying present and grounded, in the here and now, that's where you'll find happiness, contentment, and the positivity that will get you unstuck."

As resistant as I was to that, and to not having a plan or knowing what was coming next, I would come to understand that there was something freeing in just being where I was. There was something powerful in trusting that our Guides had us, our healing and our best interests, always at the forefront of their words, their actions and their asks. By not sharing the plan, they were asking us to believe in them, to believe in the process, to believe in each other and to believe in ourselves. We were being given permission to just stop and be in whatever moment was happening. And that was such a gift. We weren't on our phones, worrying about replying to emails, or work or family stressors, or all the millions of things that demand our energy every single day. We weren't finding other things to numb our emotions, or quelch our thoughts, or occupy our time and attention. For these sacred handful of days, we were focused on the moment, and on how we, as a group that started out as strangers but morphed into an enduring lifeline to one another long after we left Camp Grace, could use our collective love, support and wisdom to heal together and find a path to peace.

But we could only get there by coming to terms with the things that seemed way too scary to face. By naming and claiming the things that had happened. And it began with story.

"[In the Coast Guard], there were so many days out at sea," I recalled in my journal, reflecting on a time when struggle was a catalyst for growth, "picking up migrants, women, children. Housing them on [the] deck [of the Cutter] and not seeing them as people with lives, histories, families. Seeing them as the Mission and needing to just get it done."

As I wrote, I thought about the souls I'd encountered out there on those deep, blue waters - the scared, emaciated, frightened eyes that stared back at me after being pulled from fish holds in leaky, stinking, waterlogged wooden boats. My hand shook as it continued to write.

"That has changed for me," I penned, seeing the faces of the nameless human beings who risked everything in hopes of a better future. "If I were now in that situation, I would treat them with more compassion and understanding for leaving their homeland, their families, their existence in search of something else."

My mind drifted back to the flight deck of the Coast Guard Cutter Steadfast. Standing stoically, my black steel-toed boots felt like they were melting into the newly laid non-skid coating as the intense equatorial sun created beads of sweat that dripped down my back. My dark blue cotton t-shirt collected the runoff before it could pool at my black webbed belt, and I could feel a slight headache starting to emerge from beneath the sweat-stained mesh baseball hat that kept my thick hair at bay.

It was my job was to search all of the women and children who were brought on board.

I snapped on the blue latex gloves, standing face-to-face with women whose wrinkly foreheads and weathered eyes told stories of deeply guarded pain. I looked for contraband, weapons and drugs as they balanced infants on their hips and soothed terrified toddlers who clung to their bruised and battered legs. I remained detached, allowing no emotion to penetrate the thick armor that I was forced to put up. Demanding outstretched arms and a widened stance so I could easily conduct the pat-downs that were standard for an external search, I methodically moved from one woman to another, purposefully disconnecting from them as I completed my task.

It was all so routine, so I never stopped to wonder WHY someone would elect to take their children, and spend days out at sea, hundreds of nautical miles away from land, in fish holds that were never meant to be occupied by anything other than the catch from the sea. Years later, those questions haunted me, as the walls of protection I erected, the ones that were supposed to keep me safe from the cruelty of human trafficking, and human suffering, came tumbling down. I realized choice may not have been part of their equation.

We called it "Migrant Interdiction."

Out there on the flight deck, as the Cutter rocked with the waves, I told myself I was just doing my job. I was serving my country. I was saving lives. What I would come to understand was that, in the middle of the Pacific Ocean, I was really battling the brutality of unchecked greed and power. And the byproducts of systems that are fed by darkness and corruption were the ones who were left voiceless, powerless, with haunted eyes and wounded hearts that had run out of options. I was at war with a patriarchal system that had told me, in so many ways, that I too would one day run out of options. For years, it made me believe that I, too, was like those women and children. I was a byproduct of a system that wanted to leave me voiceless and powerless. But, here, in this space, I was learning to step into a different role, where I elected to take ownership of my actions so I could, eventually, step away from a construct that had kept me small for too many years.

Back at Camp Grace, the autumn weather provided the warmth my soul craved, as it permeated through the layers of sadness, grief and overwhelm that had calcified over the years. I learned how to create habits that would lead to “owning my morning,” and small actions I could take to empty the rucksack of hurt, guilt, shame and grief that I had been carrying for decades.

“For years,” I wrote, “I lived with the idea that I’m broken, and that something is wrong with me. That I’m different and that no one gets it. It never occurred to me to make the connection between how I was trained to be and how I currently am.”

Lightbulb.

In that week, I learned to seek support, finally understanding that we are a culmination of the three to five people we spend the most time with. And I put words to actions so I could seek out the resources I would need to move forward with my life goals.

One afternoon, we were summoned to a parking lot, where bright white pieces of paper had been laid out on the concrete. There were black numbers, drawn with markers on each piece of paper, representing ages that spanned from birth to near end-of-life, in increments of five.

One by one, we took turns, starting from the piece of paper that most closely represented our current age, to move into our future and declare, without pretense or inhibition, what we wanted out of the life that lay in front of us.

As I stood near the “50” mark, but not yet on it, I declared out loud, to myself, my Guides and my new tribe of Warrior Women, “At 50, I’ll travel to Christmas Island and launch a podcast.” Then I took the step and stood next to the “50” paper.

“At 55, I’ll learn to row the drift boat and incorporate rowing into my fly fishing classes.” Another step forward, as the voices cheered me on.

"At 60, I'll write and publish a book, lead retreats, and retire from my current job." The movement continued along with the audible encouragement that sparked an energy in my soul.

"At 65, that book will be a New York Times bestseller, I'll give TED Talks and I'll own a beach house."

My feet kept moving along my lifeline, declaring each set of new dreams and goals with more passion, excitement and a rising sense of purpose.

"At 70 I'll hike the Appalachian Trail (in segments.) At 75 I'll finish the Appalachian Trail, write a second book and, at 80, I'll travel through Tuscany by bike."

"Take us!" shouted Stacy, one of my PATHH Sisters, from the sidelines, and I smiled knowing that I didn't have to do this walk alone.

As I approached the last mark, I paused, stopping to look behind me and take in all of the visions, dreams, actions and results that I just spoke life into. I glanced at all the sheets of paper that represented a long, radiant, beautiful second half of my journey. And I thought about all the people who would walk alongside and who already had been part of my story.

"At 90," I said, catching my breath and taking time to soak in the promise of the possibility of all that lay ahead, and the finality that this statement represented, "I'll sit on my porch, with the man I love, knowing that it was worth giving love, giving life, another chance."

I examined my foundation - my values, beliefs and morals - and thought about how much of what I visioned connected with my authentic self. As I thought about what would bring me joy, and how I could transcend my circumstances to create a more aligned life for myself, I realized that the things I had stated were actually things I wanted to do. They were more than passing dreams. These were things that held great importance to me because they housed my purpose and aligned with my new mission statement. And, I would come to understand that, when we walk in our purpose, guided by our North Star, nothing seems too big, too audacious or too unattainable. After all, those things that are embedded in our hearts are the things we are meant to bring to the world.

In my reflection that evening, I wrote, "As I'm moving into the second half of life, it's so important for me to focus on the people in my life and my current being – not who I was or the trauma I went through – to cultivate the experiences, opportunities and life I want for these next chapters."

But we have to have struggles in order to have self-discovery. To be able to grow, we have to feel discomfort. Warrior PATHH pushed me to face a lot of scary things, to fully put myself out there, to do things I wasn't sure I was qualified to do, to quelch my never-ending criticism, and to push forward, knowing I was supported by people whom I would come to love like family.

With each challenge, activity, reflection, there was an opportunity for transformation. I was learning to challenge the stories I'd been telling myself and challenge my internal narratives to see if they were grounded in truth, or in fear. So, when we were asked to walk the labyrinth, I was given the gift of being able to lay those false narratives to rest. Since I'd never walked a labyrinth before, I wasn't attuned to the ancient practice of Releasing, Receiving and Returning. One step, a few tears, a slow release of the parts of my life that were keeping me stuck. Another step, more tears, and another slow release of more hidden trauma. The releasing was like the slow drip of the IV, measured, calculated, steady. I could feel myself actively shedding the burdens that had plagued me for a very, very long time. Burdens that showed up as lack of worth, lack of purpose.

Every movement of my feet meant I was both literally and figuratively stepping towards a new path. With each step I moved closer towards the center. My center. In this simple practice, I was shedding thoughts and distractions, quieting my mind and allowing myself to be open to receiving whatever was meant for me in this experience.

As I slowly made my way through the ancient maze, the misperceptions shattered into a million tiny pieces, taking with them all of the guilt, shame, self-deprecation and anger that I'd harbored for decades. And, as I made my way back out of the labyrinth, returning from the center to where I had started, I could feel that something profound had shifted. While I had been open to receiving wholeness, healing, and peace, it occurred to me that there were many other women, some in my circles and some whom I had not yet met, who needed to be in that labyrinth too. But they weren't because maybe they didn't know how to be, or maybe they didn't know that it was available. And, that stark realization reinvigorated my reason for getting into the arena in the first place.

"Breath. Nature. Grounding. Connecting with my WHY. There is something resoundingly beautiful," I would write later that evening, "about sharing space in that labyrinth with six other women who have made a conscious choice to lead the lives they are meant to live."

But it troubled me that this experience seemed to be more of an exception than the norm. Why weren't all women having these profound experiences? And that's when I knew that my fears could no longer dictate my actions. Despite being terrified of putting myself all the way out there, for people to critique, criticize and pick apart, I knew that healing starts with story and it was up to me to create a space where women could share theirs without judgement. So, when I got back to Montana, I finally launched the *Two Gals and a Mic* podcast, knowing that I was ready to share myself with the world because I knew these stories mattered.

The Art Of Courage

"Find the audacity to court tomorrow with all of its fearsome mysteries, and you will have discovered the art of courage."
- Kimberly Shumate

After returning from Georgia, I continued to explore what it would look like to lean more fully into a relationship. For the last year, I had been dipping my toes back into the dating pool, trying to reestablish my connective rhythms in a way that did not replicate the disastrous outcomes I'd experienced in South Carolina.

I hated the online scene, because I never quite knew who was real, who was honest, and who was invested for the right reasons. But meeting J.P. at a bar hadn't panned out either. Stuck between a rock and a hard place, online dating seemed like the most viable option. With an abundance of caution, I approached the online conversation I was having with a man named Josh.

Our discourse was touch-and-go, as it seemed he was fed up and frustrated with the online scene. I couldn't blame him. I was right there too. I'd spent the last year swiping right, going on dates, and being told I was "rough around the edges," and too independent – which was surprising because that's what guys said they wanted, until it was staring them down from across a high-top table at a bar offering 25-cent chicken wings on Mondays. There was so much implied judgment that came with assessing someone, in 10 seconds or less, based on a few pictures and how witty, engaging, and aligned their profile seemed, in a few key snippets that offered a quick look behind the kimono.

Josh's bio was slim. His pictures were terrible, and it was hard to ascertain exactly what he looked like because some of the snapshots were taken from a distance. There was one close-up of him holding a fish, as he sat in a drift boat and beamed.

"*Ahhh...the requisite fish picture,*" I thought. "*Why do all these dudes do that?*" It was Montana, after all, but it seemed like a man's dating summary was incomplete without at least one fishing or hunting photo.

When I first read through Josh's synopsis, I was inclined to swipe left. He didn't strike me as someone who would match what I thought I wanted in a long-term partner. However, as my index finger readied itself to discard his profile and move on, my brain signaled it to stop.

"*Huh.*" I noticed a slight fire in my belly. "*That's weird.*" The automated left swipe was replaced with something almost primeval that was telling me to swipe right and put Josh into the maybe-we-should-have-a-conversation category. Despite the lackluster photos and the dismal write-up, I listened to that glimmer and gave Josh a shot.

Our first date included a film festival followed by drinks and light conversation. It went better than a lot of the other dates I'd been on in the previous months, but overall, I was feeling discouraged and disheartened. I just couldn't seem to find someone whom I connected with on a deeper level. I was searching for the person I could invest in and who would hold my heart, dreams and desires with the respect and admiration they deserved. I wanted a partner who would be in it for the long-haul, and who wasn't looking for the Peter Pan lifestyle of playing, partying and pretending. And, while Josh was nice, I couldn't get an accurate read, which made me feel unclear and uneasy about his intentions. He would later tell me that his hesitation came from a long series of being disappointed and deserted as he went through his own dating experiences.

"You know," he shared when we had established that kind of trust, "I thought you'd ghosted me after we first started talking online."

"What?" I asked incredulously, knowing how adamant I was about cutting things off cleanly with people, and offering a proper explanation instead of just leaving them hanging out to dry.

"When you went to Austin for Christmas, I could see that the little icon on your profile said you were in Texas. So, I thought you lived there. I figured you'd only been visiting Montana for the holidays, and I fully expected you to stop talking to me."

"Are you serious?" I asked. But I couldn't blame his assessment of the situation. The online dating world is a bit like the Wild West, full of savory and unsavory people who bring in a host of different intentions and desired outcomes. It was easy to get caught up in the gaminess of it all, so having boundaries helped avoid unintended consequences.

"Well, I'm sure glad I took the chance on giving you my number," I told him. "And even more grateful you agreed to that second date."

A few weeks after the film festival, I called Josh and asked him if he wanted to accompany me to Yellowstone National Park. I had been advised that it wasn't a good idea to venture out into the backcountry alone, and I wanted to go on a cross-country skiing adventure. In the long term, I was looking for an adventure buddy, but I knew I'd have to test those waters slowly.

"Hey," I said as he picked up the phone after a few rings. "I was just calling to see if you would at all be interested in going cross-country skiing with me in Yellowstone this weekend?"

"Um…" Josh paused as he formulated his answer.

I cut him off. "I've heard the Park is beautiful in the winter, but I've also been told it's not a good idea to go out there alone. Do you want to come?" So much for altruism.

"Listen Sue," he said. I braced myself for the rejection that I knew was coming. Why was it so hard to find a companion to do these things with?

"I'm old, I'm fat and I haven't skied in 30 years. I would love to come!"

This was not the reply that I was expecting.

"I'll see you on Saturday!" A combination of smitten and shock colored my words.

It was early morning when I heard the performance muffler from his Toyota Tundra pull into my driveway. We made fast work of loading the discounted cross-country skis I'd picked up at ski swap, my boots, poles, and a swimsuit (just in case we wanted to hit the hot springs on the way home) into the bed of the truck and then we headed south on our 80-mile road trip to Yellowstone National Park. On the way, we stopped in Gardner, at the local fly fishing shop, to get Josh set up with rental gear. Grabbing coffee, we then continued through the Roosevelt Arch, past Mammoth Springs, and over to Tower Falls, where we readied ourselves for the 5-mile round-trip expedition. As Montana tends to be in late January, the morning air was nippy, so Josh and I donned layer after layer of warm weather gear, covered our heads, ears, necks and eyes, and then hit the trail. As I loped along, a small uphill grade was developing, keeping me from gaining any significant forward momentum. In fact, I found myself moving backwards, unable to get purchase beneath my skis, and fighting through the soft snow to not lose all of the ground I had just fought to gain.

As I looked over to my right, I noticed Josh was firmly in the groomed tracks, plodding along, no cares in the world, as his head moved side-to-side, taking in the rocky formations and varying landscapes that had remained steadfast and unwavering for eons. I took deep breaths, trying to stave off the frustration that was mounting. For every two glides forward, my skis, coupled with the increasing grade, would propel me five steps backwards. "Swoosh. Swoosh. Swoosh." The snow glided under the skis' waxed bottoms, and it didn't take me long to realize that I was using the wrong kind of skis for Yellowstone's varied terrain. There was no way that I was going to be able to make it through this entire expedition.

Standing in this vast wilderness, I had to make a choice. I could admit to this man whom I barely knew, that I was frustrated by my ill performing gear, and embarrassed by my inability to continue with this epic outdoor adventure – one that I had suggested – because, in my own inexperience, I had purchased the wrong equipment. Or, I could say nothing and, instead, have a meltdown, create a scene and wreck the entire date because nothing seemed to be going according to plan. I decided to go with the first option.

"Josh," I said, "I'm having some issues."

He smiled, a wide, calming grin, that was vastly different from the toothy troll's grimace that I had encountered years earlier.

"What's up?" Josh asked, as he unclipped from his skis and came over to me.

"It's my skis," I said, looking down with loathing at the pair I had purchased only a few months earlier. "I keep sliding backwards and, at this rate, there's no way I'm going to be able to make it to the Falls." I felt deflated.

"No worries," he said, as his hands reached into his pockets, and started digging around. He had gone to school for engineering, and, I would quickly come to find out, had a problem-solving, logical outlook that helped bring order to the chaos.

He pulled out the straps that were normally used to keep the skis together during transport. "We can just use this to secure them to your backpack, and we can either head back or keep going. It's whatever you want to do."

I knew he was sincere. He had no expectations. No ulterior motives. Just a guy, out with a gal, in Montana's serene outdoor playland. I met his smile with one of my own and, in a moment that felt as wild as our surroundings, I strapped the skis to my pack, threw it on my back, and headed up the mountain to find Tower Falls.

We plodded along, identifying landmarks that looked like good stopping points for quick breaks. "How about that rock up there?" Josh asked at one point, as his outstretched index finger identified a brown mass that was to the right of the trail about 100 yards in the distance.

"Perfect!" I said, excited to get to that temporary stopping point so I could readjust my pack, catch my breath and grab a snack. Hiking uphill in the snow really was hard work!

As we approached, the massive brown mass stood up, looked at us, and sauntered off.

"Oh my God!" I screeched, half terrified because we had misidentified a bison for a rock, and half amused by the absurdity of it all.

The two of us stood at the place where the bison had been, tears of laughter streaking our faces, our spirits tethered in this moment of pure joy. Laughter echoed off the canyon walls as I welcomed these new feelings of delight and excitement.

I took a minute to catch my breath and then asked, "Do you want to hit the hot springs after we finish?"

"Sounds good," he said. "It'll feel good to shake off the chill."

"For sure." I answered. And then I paused, looking him right in the eye. "But…no judgment." My hands circled around my middle-aged, ever-expanding waistline, hips and butt, areas of my body that would soon be exposed, in a swimsuit, with this guy whom I was still getting to know.

"Sue," he said, as he pointed to his mid-section, which had produced the big belly laughs just a few moments ago. "We're good." And, without any further words, Josh smiled even larger, turned and continued down the trail.

Less than a year after our Yellowstone experience, and about a year before I headed to Georgia, Josh and I found ourselves buying a home together, remodeling the entire thing, and then, shortly after moving in, pursuing our first saltwater fly fishing adventure to Cuba.

He had never been on an international trip, but Josh was a trooper and always up for a good adventure. And it was during that Cuba trip, after the airline had lost all our luggage, and we had no way to purchase any replacement items, that I saw Josh's beautiful, calm spirit arise in an entirely different way.

Our first day out on the boat, it didn't take long for the lost luggage to be forgotten and the joy to start flowing.

"I got one!" Josh exclaimed within 20 minutes of wetting our lines. His broad shoulders were squared up against the horizon as he braced himself on the bow of the skiff and watched the silvery rocket ascend from the water, into the air, and then back down into the deep blue abyss.

"Retrieve, retrieve," our guide called out excitedly, indicating that Josh needed to keep all slack out of his fly line to get the monster to the boat.

Josh wasn't nearly as animated as I tend to be as he played that fish. He followed the guide's sparse instructions, and then, without much more ballyhooing, landed the first tarpon of the trip, and his first ever saltwater fish.

It took me another six days, several failed attempts, and a relentless desire to secure one before I finally landed my first, and only, tarpon. Josh had been patient, encouraging, and upbeat as I tried, and failed, day after day.

"You'll get it," he would tell me as I nursed my virgin pina coladas at the hotel bar every evening.

"I know," I would counter, trying to meet his enthusiasm, but silently growing more and more heartbroken that I wouldn't land this coveted beauty.

It was the last cast, on the last day, when the stars aligned and I finally brought a "Silver King" to the boat. But it wasn't without an extraordinary amount of tomfoolery as my rod came apart mid-fight, and, after shoving the sections back together, realizing the guides were facing the sky, instead of the boat deck, which made playing the fish a whole lot harder.

After several minutes, and tarpon aerial acrobatics, I finally brought the fish to the boat.

"Josh!" I yelled as I stayed laser-focused on my fly line. "Grab my phone! Take some video!"

"On it!" he responded as he picked up the hard case. Pushing the camera icon in the bottom right corner, it didn't take long for him to see that something was wrong.

"It's not working," he said, as he pointed the phone's external lens in my direction.

"What do you mean it's not working?" I couldn't take the phone from his hands and see for myself, because I didn't want to risk losing that beautiful fish that was at the end of my line.

"It says you're out of memory."

"WHAT?" I screamed incredulously. "How can I be out of memory?"

"Maybe you took too many pictures of my tarpon," Josh joked.

"Now is not the time," was all I had in me to reply with.

We never got the photo, but "we go for tarpon" and "we try" – two phrases that our guide told me day after day – are now formidable phrases that Josh and I say to one another when we are facing difficult or uncertain outcomes. And those phrases always make us giggle.

As Josh and my relationship continued to grow, so did our love for adventure, trying new things and pushing each other past our perceived limits to experience a full and complete life together. Josh made me feel safe. He made me feel heard, appreciated and understood. I no longer felt abandoned, uncertain, or alone, because I had connected with myself in a way that allowed me to deeply connect with him. Which is why, on December 26, 2024, I was ready to finally stare my fear in the face and do what I didn't think was possible. I was ready to experience the Art of Courage.

As I stood on the windswept beach in Maui, under the 10 a.m. sun, I looked around at the rustic trees that bore no leaves but found solace in the ocean's waves. We landed back in Hawai'i two days earlier, returning from a week-long fly fishing adventure to Christmas Island. I was excited, giddy even, about being able to be literally stranded on an island in the South Pacific with the man I loved, fulfilling that promise I'd made on the pavement that afternoon in Georgia, when I'd proclaimed that, by 50, I would travel to Christmas Island. It would have been romantic, even a little Earnest Hemmingway, if we both hadn't contracted the Nora Virus on the plane ride there.

Within 24 hours of our arrival, we both were sicker than dogs, unable to keep anything in our bodies. We had been advised that there really weren't medical facilities on the island, so we packed a variety of medical supplies and brought with us some creature comforts of home. But, with the Noro Virus, the only thing to do was stay hydrated and wait it out. So, we leaned into the experience, and each other, and found joy in the moments when we felt well enough to walk the volcanic beaches and saltwater flats, in search of colorful fish. We chased Permit, Bluefin Trevally, Bonefish and Triggerfish, filling our days catching and releasing tropical species that looked like they belonged in an aquarium.

I knew that any man who would willingly hold my hair while rubbing my back and giving me water, as I violently wretched on the bathroom floor, was genuinely in it with me. I knew I could count on Josh, no matter what circumstances life threw our way. And, as odd as it sounds, it was in that very unpleasant, and quite humiliating moment, that I knew, without hesitation, that Josh was indeed my forever person.

So, as I stood with him on this beach in Maui and adjusted the Lei Po'o that sat as a crown atop of my wavy silver strands, I sighed deeply. Lavender roses, white orchids, purple thistles and green tea leaves, to match the tea leaf lei that adorned Josh's neck, created a statement of gentle wildness that exemplified the Warrior Woman whom I had allowed myself to become. My gauzy cream dress, which stopped just short of my ankles, whispered in the breeze, as the golden-hued flowers on its fabric came as alive as I felt. Josh's plum-colored linen shirt and khaki linen shorts gave space for his large frame to breathe, and shifted slightly in the sand, as his back faced the waves and his eyes locked into mine.

"It's taken me a really long time to believe in love again," I started, as I grasped Josh's large hands, feeling the cool sand shift slightly under my varnished toes. "And an even longer time to want to commit to it." I could feel myself slowly settling into the safety of his presence. Never, in a million years, did I think I would ever have the courage to marry again. Yet, here I was, in a simple beach elopement, feeling like all time had stopped and the only thing that mattered was us, together. "Thank you for being incredibly patient and kind as I worked through my process so I could finally land in this beautiful place where love looks and feels different. The love my heart holds for you is more complex than I've ever known," I continued. "It's Richer. Deeper. Fearless and Enduring because it's cultivated by the understanding, respect and compassion that we hold for one another. Our love is a gift, and I am so grateful to fully embrace it, to fully embrace you, and to fully embrace our life together. I don't know what God has in store for us. But I do know that the journey will be epic, and absolutely amazing, as long as we both continue to say yes to Him, and yes to each other. From saltwater adventures to mountain experiences, with you by my side, as partners, as equals, as husband and wife, there's no other person I can imagine navigating this second half with."

Without missing a beat, Josh replied with the words he had written from his heart to mine.

"I, Josh, take you, Sue, for this wonderful adventure of life." he said. "From little afternoon hot springs adventures all the way to week-long, no-way-out adventures, I promise to love you, support you, and never take you for granted." My eyes teared up as he continued. "I am so blessed God has given your love to me and will always cherish you. It has taken me half my life to find you and now that I have, I am never letting you go. I love you and want to experience our greatest adventure for the rest of our lives!"

Simple, yet incredibly impactful – just like him.

It was hard to imagine that, eight years earlier, I had been alone, on a cold South Carolina beach, where I walked uncertain, unhinged, unloved. Now as I stood in the warm mid-morning breeze on this Maui paradise, absent of all the judgement and pretense, Josh took my heart, and all that came with it. He created a safe space for me to find refuge and gave me the runway to continue to grow and expand as a bold, beautiful woman. As peace and certainty settled deep within my bones, I settled into myself and my Warrior Woman spirit. I had reclaimed my voice and followed the glimmers which led me home, to him.

Part II:
Arriving

My Own Fork In The Road

"A ship in harbor is safe, but that's not what ships are built for."

- John A. Shedd

If I'd known what lay ahead as we entered 2025, I would have elected to stay rooted on that beach in Maui, with my toes in the sand, and my hands firmly grasping Josh's big paws. But that's not how life goes. As the next year would unfold, I would be tested in ways I could never have imagined. I would be placed in positions where the choice to use my voice became more important than staying quiet, where my Warrior Woman would be the bright beacon of hope in a world that would be absolutely flipped upside down, and, where the glimmers were the only things that offered direction during a time when nothing made sense. I would question my deservedness as I pursued purpose with wild abandon, and discover that, like the starfish, I could adapt and evolve as I traversed through the chaos. The strongest steel and most brilliant diamonds are forged in the hottest of fires. Whether I knew it or not, I was sharpened, shining and ready for battle. I had arrived.

Working for the federal government was supposed to be safe. It was enough, until it wasn't. One week after Inauguration Day, 2025, I traveled to the U.S. Fish and Wildlife's National Conservation Training Center (NCTC) in Shepherdstown, West Va. to kick off a year-long advanced leadership program. As our group gathered for our first in-person residency in the "Eagles Nest" building, aptly named because of its proximity to the two nests that had been built on platforms in the nearby trees, I committed to taking the next year to explore, and experience what deep and profound change would look and feel like when I put it into action.

On that first morning, writing my name on the dry erase placard, I thought about how I wanted to show up not only for these fourteen days, but for the remainder of the year. How could I find my place in this complex web of people who harbored backgrounds and experiences vastly different from my own? What impact did I want to have? What legacy did I want to leave?

"*Alrighty Sue,*" I thought as I looked around the room. The faces, staring back, were of complete strangers who, like me, had been selected to attend this prestigious program. We hailed from across the Service, bringing a myriad of experience, opinions and world views. But we were all anchored in our love of the natural world, and our commitment to conservation. "*No one knows you. How do you want to show up for this experience?*"

I had a chance to explore this question in one of our first getting-to-know-you activities. Gathered in small groups, we were each invited to draw our lifelines, using pictures in lieu of words to represent major events and circumstances that happened from birth until present day. While the directions stated we needed to focus at least half of the timeline on the first 20 years, I wrestled with the idea of sharing the more seminal events that had happened within the last eight. As I joined a small contingency of my colleagues in a breakout room, I stared at the large, empty paper.

"*How much should I share?*" I thought as I observed the blank canvas. I picked up a marker from the table and rolled it between my thumb and forefinger. "*I mean, if I share all my crazy, are these folks going to think I'm totally unhinged?*" I looked around the table, seeing others in my group already drawing their pictures.

It would have been easy to stay superficial and create simple symbols to identify my sibling relationships, going to Catholic school, singing in church choir and being a voracious bookworm. But what about the parts of me that better defined the woman whom I'd become? My time in Africa and in the Coast Guard. My Ironman finish. The hospitalization. Sobriety. Clawing my way back after falling over the cliff. TMS. Becoming a fly fishing instructor. And, taking a chance on myself by moving to Montana, where I met Josh and learned that love can be safe and enduring. What about all of those highlights? I weighed my options and considered the importance of story and truth, how safety factored into using my voice with purpose and precision, and how to balance what I wanted to say with what I needed to say.

With a new administration, work no longer felt like a safe place to express any modicum of vulnerability or authenticity. Executive Order 14151, signed January 20, 2025, demanded "the termination of all discriminatory programs, including illegal DEI and 'diversity, equity, inclusion, and accessibility' (DEIA) mandates, policies, programs, preferences, and activities in the Federal Government, under whatever name they appear." As a result of that mandate, I'd spent several days filtering through websites and other communication materials before I departed for West Virginia, erasing my own work products to ensure they no longer included any mention of Diversity, Equity or Inclusion.

It was a painstaking process, and certainly not something I agreed with. But, I complied and, just when I thought I was done, I was advised that the *Nature's Infrastructure* podcast, which I'd spent the previous year writing, coordinating, recording, editing and publishing, had to also be erased because the conservation-based conversations I'd had with partners and Tribal nations no longer aligned with the administration's priorities. In broad strokes, I saw three years' worth of my time, my diligence, my expertise and my efforts erased. Programs were being cancelled. Voices were being cancelled. I was being cancelled. And, like my Warrior Woman Spirit who showed up during TMS, I was pissed.

But it wasn't until Executive Order 14168, that was entitled "Defending Women from Gender Ideology Extremism and Restoring Biological Truth to the Federal Government," was implemented that I became unglued. By weaponizing gender and women's safety, this policy opened the door to broader discrimination, hurt an already vulnerable population, ignored the complexity of what it means to be a woman (whether biologically or through self-identification) and created the opportunity for increased societal harm. The motivation behind this policy was based in the same toxic bias that I'd faced my entire career. It was the subtle discrimination I'd encountered when defending women's health to The Mayor. The same overlording that came from men in Ethiopia who defended genital mutilation as a patriarchal value, despite it being ruled illegal shortly after I returned stateside. Deeply rooted in cultural norms, some Ethiopian men condoned the practice of partially or completely removing women's external genitalia as a way to protect women's societal status, marriageability and meet religious requirements. I had seen, first-hand, how damaging it was to create a sweeping policy to address what was clearly a personal decision. Nothing about this Executive Order made me believe it would protect and defend women, as the title indicated. After surviving military sexual trauma, gender discrimination, and a litany of microaggressions over the years, I wasn't interested in kowtowing to a policy that wanted to define what it meant for me – or anyone else – to be female.

Yet, despite the vitriolic rhetoric that was being espoused from the belly of our nation's capital, I wasn't going to let fear get the best of me. And I wasn't going to perpetuate the grossly misrepresented ideology of federal workers that was playing out in the news cycles. I worked alongside highly intelligent, dedicated, diligent people who didn't deserve to be lumped into a political narrative that painted all federal workers as lazy. We chose to serve our country through Civil Service for different reasons. But, despite the impetus for joining the federal workforce, most had opted to stay not because of the pay, but because of the positive impact of their life's work. In the field of conservation, positive impact could literally be the difference between the restoration or the extinction of a species. The stakes are high because once a species is extinct, it's gone forever. And no one wants to be responsible for that outcome.

So, as I looked at the blank white paper and the marker I was still holding, I thought about my own story. I considered the boundaries I needed to create to remain safe in this volatile environment and balanced that need with all of the trials and tribulations I'd had to overcome to even be standing in that room.

Whether or not my lifeline resonated with my audience was no longer important. What was important was that my story mattered. My voice mattered. And I had the power and authority to decide what that looked like – as a leader, as a friend, as a Warrior Woman, as Sue – in any setting or circumstance. I knew that I needed to stand in my truth because I had come too far to let that be erased. I wanted to share just to see what would happen if I went deeper than what people could see on the surface. "*What would it look like,*" I thought, "*if I exposed my starfish underbelly and shared the squishy, messy parts that I was too afraid to let people see?*" I thought about the associated risks, knowing that every decision has a tradeoff. "*Those pieces of me played such a big role in who I am now. And, I can't work in an environment where I can't be who I am. All of who I am,*" I reminded myself. "*Be brave, Sue. Take the chance.*"

I leaned in and started drawing, purposefully, with bold, brazen strokes, creating a symbolic representation of the messy, yucky, icky aspects that had historically been reserved for healing retreats and therapy sessions. Tiny pictures littered the paper as the complexity of my lived human experience took shape. This was the first time I'd allowed my *Gentle Fucking Flower* and *Battle Axe* to emerge collectively in a professional setting, and I was more than a little anxious to see how that would be received.

After we completed our drawings, we were asked to share the stories behind each of those representative icons within our small groups. I hung my paper on the whiteboard, took a deep, cleansing breath, and began.

Pointing to each of the markings on the paper, I gave honest, unfiltered insight into the highs and lows that life had offered through the course of 50 years. My colleagues listened, with interest and curiosity, and then gave hugs and encouragement when I was finally finished. In return, they also offered their honest stories, and all the highlights, lowlights and the messy in-betweens of what their journeys had entailed. It was a victory of epic proportions because, in my refusal to be quieted, or shy away, I gained the safety and acceptance that I'd been seeking and gave that in return.

So, when the first Deferred Resignation Program (DRP) was offered a few days later, which was notoriously dubbed as the "Fork in the Road," I opted out. My colleagues had provided an oasis of hope, and, with their help, I was certain I would weather this storm.

As I thought about that turning point, I understood that I was at my own Fork in the Road. Outside of this little bubble, I no longer had the same ability to use my voice or the opportunity to do the type of work I'd been engaged in for nearly two decades. I had already seen how quickly my previous efforts had been erased, and I wasn't interested in putting more of my valuable time and thought equity into stories, interviews or communications that would end up on the cutting room floor. But I still had agency outside of the office. So, I created space for my curious mind to tinker. I uplifted and honored creative and diverse ideas and included people who bravely, boldly, and unapologetically showed up. I began to dig into the glimmers that surfaced, small at first but larger as the year went on. My intuitive love language was asking me to move past the luxury of playing it safe and into the uncomfortable spaces of the unknown. I was led to expand myself and my skills in ways I hadn't yet considered and nudged to do work that I had never felt equipped to do.

As I worked to put these notions into motion, a plan began to form. It became more than evident that, in a time when voices, histories and entire truths were being erased, my purpose was to create space for the opposite outcomes. I doubled down on my personal efforts because, as evidenced with the *Two Gals and a Mic* podcast, the collective is a powerful force. And, when a powerful force is anchored in love and compassion, instead of hate and divisiveness, it can overcome even the darkest of circumstances.

Five Bullets

"Lead by example with hope, never fear."
– Michelle Obama

A few weeks following the Fork in the Road's deadline, mass federal layoffs began. The iconic image of the Department of Government Efficiency's head honcho, the man in black, wielding a chainsaw with the words "Long live liberty, damn it" emblazoned on the blade that hung high in the air, littered my social media feeds. DOGE was slashing everything in its path with reckless abandon. The bloodbath had started on February 12, peaked on Valentine's Day, and been codified into a formalized directive, with a memo from the Office of Personnel Management on February 17, which directed Federal agencies to fire certain probationary employees by the end of the day.

There was a hurricane circling around me, sweeping up everything in its destructive path. I was in the eye of the storm, so, when my phone rang as I was headed into the grocery store on a Saturday afternoon, I stopped dead in my tracks, wondering why my Washington D.C.-based boss lady would be calling me on my personal cell phone line.

"Hey, Sue."

She rarely called me after work hours, and, when she did, it was never on my personal line. I could almost smell the rotisserie chicken that beckoned from behind the sliding glass doors. If only I'd made it past the threshold, into the safety of the grocery store, before answering the phone. But, alas, now I was stuck, rooted in place, feeling heavy with the weight of what she was about to say, like the branches of the trees that surrounded me, wet with snow from the night before.

"*Shit,*" I thought, as humiliation hit me hard. I was about to lose my dignity, and my job, on the icy asphalt of a Safeway parking lot.

"Hi," I said, trying to keep my tone chipper.

"Listen. We just received word about needing to submit five bullet points each Monday to summarize your weekly accomplishments."

"What?" I was not following the conversation, and my mind was still waiting for her to say, "And, oh yeah, you're fired." That last sentence never materialized.

"We don't have much more information. We're trying to understand if this is legitimate or not, so I wanted to call in case you see something in the news. I'll let you know when I hear something more."

I thanked her but couldn't figure out why this warranted a phone call on a Saturday. And then, as I walked through those sliding glass doors and into the warmth of the grocery store, I opened Reddit. Controversy had erupted in the *FedNews Feed*, with a whole slew of questions and commentary from anonymous posts, all pointing back to the head of DOGE's Tweet that said, "failure to respond [comply] would be taken as a resignation."

"*This definitely calls for ice cream,*" I thought as I headed directly to the frozen food aisle. I mean, what alternate universe had I entered to be told that, after almost two decades of service to this country, keeping my job hinged on an ultimatum posted to Twitter? What in the name of God was happening? I thought about the tidbit my boss had shared. *"You'll need to submit five bullet points each Monday to summarize your weekly accomplishments."* As I reviewed the contents of the previous five days in my mind's eye, I could feel the heat rise in my neck and cheeks.

"*You want to know what I did last week?*" I picked up the frozen pint of chocolate peanut butter swirl, hoping the coolness of it in my hands would temper my anger as I recalled the oath I'd taken when I entered civil service. "*I spent my week solemnly supporting and defending the Constitution of the United States against all enemies, foreign and domestic; bearing true faith and allegiance to the same; taking this obligation freely, without any mental reservation or purpose of evasion; and faithfully discharging the duties of the office on which I have entered. What did you do you stupid mother-"*

The internal diatribe was cut short as my phone buzzed with an incoming text message from one of my girlfriends who was also a federal employee.

"I am just blown away," she said. And then added, "I hope we get some guidance on what to respond with."

"*Yeah, me too,*" I thought.

Over the next week, direction was scarce, but questions were abundant. *Were we supposed to include sensitive or classified information in our responses? How detailed did these bullets need to be? Who would be reading the bullets and how would the information be used?*

"I haven't heard a thing from my supervisor," my girlfriend confirmed five days after the Safeway incident. "We are operating business as usual and pretending the dumpster fire around us isn't happening. It's bizarre."

She wasn't wrong. The entire year had been bizarre as the shoes continued to drop. First it was erasure. Then toxic purging of qualified and dedicated professionals. Now thinly veiled threats over very public social media channels. And, amongst all of it, there was no leadership, no guidance, no one to light the path.

I thought back to the last eight years, and how a lack of communication, transparency and openness could lead to isolation and a sense of desperation that was crippling. But I also thought about the antithesis of that, and what happened when I sought mentors to show me the way. As people entered into or dropped out of my life, the unsettling reality was that not everyone would be excited for my change. Some who had known me as broken, discouraged and downtrodden didn't know how to relate to me as I became whole, empowered and hopeful. I set boundaries to indicate my new playing field, and the new rules that would define this new territory. Some people were interested; others were not. Most let me know. But, there was also the small contingency of friends and colleagues who elected, on their own, to move on as my growth progressed, and they forgot, or intentionally decided not to let me know. And those relationship failures hurt the most.

What I knew I needed in this dark night of the soul was badass friends, like my *Two Gals* community, who would hold space for my hopes and dreams, and remind me that I had everything I needed to stay the course. Whether I was met with dogma, demons or deterrents, I needed trusted supporters, like my leadership program cohort members, my PATHH sisters, and Josh, who were unafraid to walk the unlit path with me. And I needed voices of reason, like Dave, my leadership program reflection partner, whom I had been randomly paired with during the in-person residency, to remind me that my faith mattered more than my fear.

"Sue," he affirmed as we were lamenting about the water-cooler rumors of an impending mass downsizing, "think about all of the things you've navigated when you didn't know the outcome. And all the times God walked beside you."

"It's crazy, right?" I acknowledged.

"So, how is this any different?"

"It just feels different." I didn't have a better answer. Just one that came from the past few months of never knowing what was going to happen next.

At the start of the year, I'd begun in earnest to put time and energy into writing a book because, almost 365 days prior to this conversation, I had been standing in my kitchen, the refrigerator light illuminating my face, when a knowingness, that felt more like a directive than an invitation, surged through me. I knew that sharing the wisdom I'd gained from the women on the podcast, coupled with parts of my own journey, could help break down barriers and give voice to things that needed to surface. In a time when the burdens felt heavy, I wanted to make a positive impact, and I wanted to be a bright torch helping to light the path.

"Dave. What would you do if you could do anything you wanted to, if you didn't have to play it safe?"

"What do you mean?"

"I mean, if this all falls apart, what would you want to do? What do you feel called to do? What brings you joy?"

"I'm not sure," he pondered. But I could see Dave's wheels turning, and I knew that there was something brewing. "What about you, Sue? What's your calling?"

"To write the book," I said matter-of-factly. "I just really, really feel like I need to share these stories. To share my story.

Something tells me that this is more than just publishing a memoir."

I thought about all the glimmers I'd followed, all the times I'd said yes without knowing the outcome, and all the times I moved with intuitive certainty despite the fear that wanted to hold me back. I didn't know yet what that declaration meant, but I was certain that clarity would come soon.

Glimmers Of Belize

"You get in life what you have the courage to ask for."
– Oprah Winfrey

We all felt that another shoe was about to fall, and it didn't take long for a second deferred resignation program, or "DRP 2.0," to hit the streets. This time, however, the options were a little different than the first Fork in the Road because the offer included voluntary early retirement for individuals who had reached at least 50 years of age and had at least 20 years of federal service time.

I was missing my years-in-service by 24 months, so accepting the DRP 2.0 would negatively affect my retirement. Yet, paid administrative leave through the end of the fiscal year, and then figuring out my "what's next," sounded really appealing. As I weighed the option to take or pass on the DRP 2.0., I knew this wasn't a decision I could make in isolation.

"Josh," I said, as we sat down to discuss it. "They just offered a second early retirement option."

"Are you going to take it?"

"Honestly, I don't know. But, I'm not sure I can do this anymore."

"Do you have to decide now?"

"There's a pretty short window," I said. "I have an additional 45 days to consider the offer before it becomes set in stone because I'm over 40. So, I guess I could put my name on the list and then take it back off before that deadline if I change my mind."

"You could." Josh agreed.

"I could," I echoed.

And then the tears fell. Tears that had been waiting for the right time to release the heartache, the loss, the grief, the pain, the frustration that came from having to step into an unexpected and uncertain future. After following glimmers for the previous eight years, my soul knew I would be ok if I decided to change my trajectory and start down this new path as an author, a coach, a fly fishing instructor, a writing teacher, or whatever else felt aligned and exciting. But, while my heart yearned to embark on bold and fanciful adventures, the practical and pragmatic parts of me wanted me to act responsibly and make it 24 more months to get the full retirement that I'd worked so hard to earn.

I was conflicted, because I wanted to honor my Warrior Woman and not give in because of doubt or fear. I thought about one of my original mentors, and undoubtedly the Greatest of All Time (G.O.A.T.) when it came to badass women in my life. Cheri' had been my supervisor when I was stationed in New Orleans during my final Coast Guard tour. She was a compassionate, strong woman who, just like in the paintings she created as an artist, had learned the art of blending. She amalgamated sharp edges with tactful, considerate delivery, exuding a command presence without the air of condescension that many senior leaders carried.

In her formative Coast Guard years, Cheri' was the first African American to become a rescue swimmer and was the only woman to complete the four-month pre-training Coast Guard course before joining one other female for the final training and certification with the U.S. Navy.

"There were the two of us [women] in a group of about 30 people," Cheri' shared on the podcast. "It was a very physically demanding job. Very challenging."

Over the course of eighteen weeks, Cheri' had to meet the same standards as her male counterparts, treading water while holding a 10-pound brick for extended periods of time, swimming 25 yard laps underwater without taking a breath, tugging a classmate through the water for up to 1.5 miles, and practicing ways to break free from a victim who, if found in a state of panic, could climb on or try to submerge their rescuer during the extraction. There were also timed runs and swims, high-repetition push-ups and sit-ups and technical training that included parachute packing and survival gear maintenance.

"One of the older instructors, who hadn't been able to make it [through the course] himself, took my classmates aside and said, 'She'll never make it.' Well, you know. That had to be proven wrong."

At 27 years old, Cheri' transformed from a woman who barely knew how to doggie paddle, to one of only five women to graduate from the Rescue Swimmer program. And, because of her monumental achievement, the Coast Guard changed the name of the 'Aviation Survival Man' rating to 'Aviation Survival Tech.'

"I look at the things women have done. Strong, phenomenal, demanding things. So, I just forged ahead. I was determined I would make it or die trying."

G.O.A.T.

"One of the biggest things I learned," Cheri' said, "was that I had untapped resources within me. I had no idea who I really was until I was pushed to that level. And I think all of us are like that. We see the surface, but we don't even know ourselves fully."

Like the starfish.

"It's incredible what you can do if you really are willing to apply and sacrifice…" Cheri's words rumbled through my brain.

"What do you want to do?" Josh asked, rousing me from reminiscing about days gone by.

"Go to Belize."

He looked at me and, without hesitation, said, "Then, do that."

"But, first, I think I'll put my name on the DRP list. You know - just in case…"

Belize had come up the previous month when I was on a women veteran's fly fishing trip in Michigan. As we floated the Pere Marquette, scouting for steelhead, we talked about our dreams and desires – the things that often stay hidden because they seem too whimsical, or too far-fetched to chase.

"I'd love to own a place in Belize," I said offhandedly. I'd been to Belize with J.P., on our honeymoon, and fallen in love with the country. When we returned to Houston, we almost bought a little beach bungalow, but it never came to fruition. And, honestly, I didn't think much more about owning a foreign property until this chilly day, when the river was ready to receive all of our far-flung ideas. "It would be so cool to run retreats there, focusing on storytelling and fly fishing and ways women can come together, be in community, and heal together." This was the first time I had spoken life to the vision that had been percolating for several weeks.

As our boat progressed along, I thought about the women in my circles who, like me, had found inspiration, fellowship, and purpose on the river. I thought about Taylor, the owner of *Frying Pan Anglers*, a fly shop in Basalt, Colorado.

"I know how powerful and healing fly fishing is, just from personal experience," she had shared on the podcast. "Just being outside, being on the water…it can only help those…heal from whatever they need healing from. It's not linear, and I think it's magical."

As I got to know Taylor, and her origin story, I found out she applied to veterinarian school and, when COVID hit, found herself waitlisted without a backup plan.

"When I didn't get into veterinary school," she told me candidly in our interview, "I just didn't know what my purpose was. I didn't know where I was supposed to go, what I was supposed to do. I think that was so hard for me. I had wanted to be a veterinarian since I was probably in the third grade. I kind of put myself in a box. So, I would say my biggest blessing was never getting into veterinary school and being waitlisted. As scary as that was, it led me to where I needed to be, and where my purpose was."

This storyline was so similar to my current predicament. I thought I was headed for Senior Executive Service within the federal system. I thought I'd do another decade of service and then maybe consider retirement. But, like Taylor's unexpected gift of being waitlisted, I was in the throes of DRPs, Forks in the Road and Five Bullet Points. And I was reassessing the likelihood of ever being able to make it to that senior of a position with the federal government, and, more importantly, if I still had the desire or interest to pursue it.

"I would argue that my purpose has found me as opposed to me finding my purpose. I think a lot of clarity has come from just taking the opportunities that are in front of you," Taylor had shared.

"*What are the opportunities that are in front of me?*" I wondered. "*And what would it look like to actually take a chance on them?*"

As Chris, my fly fishing guide, moved the oars to navigate around a log that was blocking the river, the boat's sudden shift aroused me back into the presence of the river and her magical beauty.

"Hey Sue," Chris said, nonchalantly, "I have a buddy in Belize who is a real estate agent. I can give you his number if you want."

"Are you serious?"

"Totally," he replied without hesitation. "You should give him a call."

I took the number and, just shy of a month later, two of my girlfriends and I boarded a plane and headed for Central America. There was a mix of relief and anxiety that hung over me like a cloud, and I thought adding my name to the DRP 2.0 list would have felt more liberating. Part of me approached the decision with finality, stating I was done and ready to move forward. But the other part knew there was a built-in safety net, and I still had time and agency to take my name off the list and choose to stay. So, I was deeply grateful to be going to Belize with two strong Warrior Women who had played important and impactful roles in my life.

When I first moved to Montana, Ashley, whom I'd met when I met Donna, invited me to ski with her. "I'm not great," I told her as I thought back to my last time on a ski slope in Colorado, which was many, many moons ago.

"It's ok," she said. "We can just go slow."

But, harkening back to the same feelings I'd had when I was learning to fly fish, I knew I didn't want to be an anchor, and I certainly didn't want to slow her down.

"Are you sure? I don't want to hold you up."

"Seriously," she said with unbridled enthusiasm. "I promise. It'll be fun."

So, I took her up on her offer and, during my first winter in Montana, we spent many blue bird days seeking powder in the tree lines, as she patiently shepherded me down terrain that she knew I could handle, but that I never, ever would have attempted on my own.

"Just don't look at the sign," she would tell me as we pointed our skis downhill. "You've got this. You totally can do this."

Choosing faith over fear, I often found myself navigating through mogul fields and tree trails, experiencing a side of myself I had never really accessed. Just like Donna and the Spartan race, Ashley helped me test my limits, push my boundaries, and lean into uncertainty with a wild sense of responsible abandon. I trusted her completely and knew she wouldn't take me down a run I couldn't recover from. She saw my capabilities and encouraged me to stop limiting myself because of my own internal narratives. And, with her tutelage and encouragement, over the course of a few seasons, ski trails that seemed inaccessible became routine.

The other woman was Tricia, whom I'd met through Bible Study. She was in a transition period and was leaning into some of the things she had shared about on her podcast episode. "I feel like I'm simplifying the things that I do," she said. "I'm putting my heart into those areas [and] I'm also learning to prioritize myself. When I prioritize what I need…the rest just falls into place. I've really embraced that I can be brave, that I can step out and do things that God puts on my heart. And, I can step out and do them in fear."

It took us almost 24 hours to reach the tropics, but as I put my toes in the sands of Belize's white beaches and stared out into the Caribbean blue waters, everything changed.

As we spent our days drinking in the calm and chasing sunsets on the golf cart, clarity crept in.

I thought about the glimmer I'd voiced on the river, with Chris as our guide. I wanted to buy a place and offer retreats that focused on storytelling and fly fishing. I knew the trade-off would be a financial one, but the way my heart swelled up with a sense of purpose and calling told me it would be 100% worth the sacrifice. "It's incredible what you can do if you really are willing to apply and sacrifice…" Cheri' had said. I was starting to see what she meant.

On our second morning, Tricia and I sat on the rooftop patio, the tops of the palm trees barely concealing the lapping waves that were hitting the nearby beach. The faint, acrid scent of sargassum floated through the air as we sipped our coffee and welcomed the day. Visions of my future self – the Warrior Woman who was writing, speaking, coaching, and leading nature-based retreats - surfaced in my mind's eye as I relaxed into the island breezes and tropical temperatures.

We spent the week looking at properties, and filling the in-between time with hammocks, mocktails and sunshine. I considered a future with Josh, on this tiny island, as we snorkeled in the Hol Chan Marine Reserve, watching turtles, nurse sharks, manta rays, and a diversity of marine life, live their best lives in this thriving ecosystem. And I thought about the life walk I'd done in Georgia, where I'd declared that, "At 50, I'll travel to Christmas Island and launch a podcast." Check and check. "At 55, I'll learn to row the drift boat and incorporate rowing into my fly fishing classes." I was still working on these. "At 60, I'll write and publish a book, lead retreats, and retire from my current job. At 65, that book will be a New York Times bestseller, I'll give TED Talks and I'll own a beach house."

As I snorkeled around this sacred space, it occurred to me that my desires may have been correct, but my timing may have been a bit off. I still wasn't sure. But what I did know was that the only way to own a beach house was to take the first step and buy a property.

I thought about what Tricia had said about bravery. "I don't have to have it all together," she had offered. "I don't have to have all the answers. But I just need to take that next step. Sometimes those steps don't make much sense."

The next day, we met up with the realtor and toured a development on Ambergris Caye.

"This neighborhood is really up-and-coming," he noted as we went from lot to barren lot in our golf carts. "There are plans to develop an airport, and a new lumber store and gas station just went in, up the road."

I glanced around, admiring the open landscape which was dotted with just a few elevated beach bungalows. The Caribbean Sea was directly in front of us when we faced east and there were new canals that were being constructed on the western side, which would open up water and boat access to the bay.

We stopped at a small lot, just a block or so from the newly forming canals. I stepped out of the golf cart and could feel my feet rooting and grounding on the small, cleared plot of land. Then I felt the glimmer. Looking up, I saw a Pacific Reef Heron perched on the bare branch of a nearby tree, and I instinctively knew that this is where future me wanted to be with future Josh, doing the future work that was placed on my heart. I'd found our landing spot.

"You have to be brave enough to just do it," Tricia had said.

Indeed.

But that bravery came with sacrifice, and I wasn't sure if sacrifice meant leaving federal service and giving up a full retirement package, or if it meant staying in and continuing to ride the rollercoaster for the next few years. I didn't have clarity as I boarded my flight home and, on the extended travel from Belize City to Denver, I mentally reviewed every scenario I could imagine to make the numbers, and the dream, work.

It was during the layover in Denver that it finally hit me. Walking through the buffet line at the United Club, as I was placing Colby and Swiss cheese cubes on my small, porcelain plate, the glimmer struck me like a lightning bolt, and I knew the buzz in my stomach was more than hunger pangs.

"Shit," I muttered under my breath. "Are you sure?" I wasn't talking to anyone in particular. Just God, and the quiet space in-between my head and my heart and the buffet glass.

I needed to talk to Josh.

"Hey," I said when he answered the phone. I didn't want to wait until I got back to Bozeman, because I knew he would be in bed, and it was important for me to process this revelation.

"Hey," his groggy voice responded. "Everything ok?"

I'd already texted him to let him know I had landed safely in Denver. I traveled quite a bit, and we used text messages to track my whereabouts because layovers could be tight, and airports were noisy. So, a phone call was quite unusual, especially when I was one flight away from being home.

"Yes," I said into the receiver. I wasn't quite sure where to go with this whole conversation. "I'm having second thoughts. I don't think it's the right time to leave."

"What changed?" he asked, perking up and now fully invested in the conversation.

I thought about this for a few seconds. Was it fear? Was it a lack of faith that we could pay for a place in Belize, and create a space for retreats and workshops, with Josh's income and whatever I made from a newly established coaching business and a book that wasn't yet in the pipeline? Was it practicality versus fantasy? Or was it simply that the timing was off?

"I don't know," I responded, because that was the easiest thing to say.

And then I made the connection that my reasons for wanting to stay had nothing to do with any of these things.

"That's not true. I do know. I guess, if I'm honest, I want to see this leadership program through to the end. I worked really hard to get here and I feel like there's more that I'm supposed to learn. I'm not sure I want to give up on that quite yet."

"That makes sense. So, what are you going to do?" Josh was always so pragmatic, yet never the one to dictate the decisions that I needed to make for myself.

"I'm not sure. But I have until tomorrow morning to figure it out."

Early the next morning, I headed into my office and powered on my work computer. I read through the emails that had accumulated during my week-long absence and homed in on the one that was entitled "Deferred Resignation Program."

I opened the electronic correspondence, reading through the legalese on the Separation Agreement that, once signed, would make my departure official. Nothing about it felt right. And, with no further deliberation, I responded to that email with one sentence.

"Please take my name off the list."

Hitting send, I audibly exhaled and then strapped in for the impending rollercoaster ride.

Within the week, Josh and I made another decision and started the acquisition paperwork for the parcel of land where my feet, and my heart, had felt deeply rooted. We were excited about becoming Belizean landowners, even though we didn't have a solid plan of how we were going to make the build happen. But that was a future problem to solve for another day. We would own land and, for now, that was enough. In time, I knew the rest of the details would work themselves out.

Part III:
Thriving

Fifty And Fearless

"Beauty begins the moment you decide to be yourself."
- Coco Chanel

"There!" Kendyl exclaimed, as the boat traversed the channel that would lead us back to the marina. I had my head in the cooler, looking for a water to take away the bad taste in my mouth. We had been at it for hours, our small skiff roaming the marshes and bayous, and we'd had no luck with bringing a fish to the boat.

Kendyl and I were in New Orleans to celebrate our 50th birthdays with Taylor Swift's "Eras" Tour and, since October is prime redfish season, we opted to spend a day fly fishing on the Mississippi Delta to see how many bulls we could wrangle into the boat.

As our fly fishing guide cruised the waters near Hopedale, Kendyl and I scouted for birds, turbulent water and any other signs that schools of redfish could be nearby. This wasn't our first expedition into unknown territory together. Kendyl, an appellate attorney, and I had met a few years earlier during a *Project Healing Waters* fly fishing retreat in Montana. As we shared time on the boat, during that retreat, and then over dinners and cozy fireplace gatherings with a few other women who were in attendance, our conversations delved into navigating well in spaces and places that were traditionally male dominated. From those initial conversations, Kendyl and I developed both a personal friendship, and a professional relationship, where we worked together with a team to curate fly fishing programming which would address the needs of women in service and who had transitioned to veteran status.

"There's an essay that I wrote that the American Bar Association published in one of their journals *Lessons for Litigators*," Kendyl had shared with me. "It is filled with thoughts about things you can take from fly fishing that have meaning in other contexts."

Over the years, I'd found many, many lessons ensconced in the art and practice of fly fishing, which is why I loved any opportunity to be on the water, chasing fish. But, on this day, I was frustrated because we had yet to find any. And I wasn't thrilled that we were going home empty handed but we both knew that it was all part of any fishing experience. Sometimes there were many, and sometimes there were none.

"There!" she yelled again, her index finger pointing at a flock of terns that were circling about 100 yards away.

Looking up, I saw the birds she was eyeing.

"I don't know," the guide sighed, with an air of defeat. I wondered if his lack of enthusiasm was indicative of an absence of fish, or his desire to be done for the day.

"What do you mean you don't know?" Kendyl asked him as she pointed again to the terns. "You said, 'look for birds.' They are right there!" She drew her index finger towards the sky, signaling our eyes again to the circling flock and leaving no room for argument.

"We can try," our guide offered half-heartedly, as he pointed the boat in their direction.

As we transited to the spot, I stepped up to the bow, pulling fly line off my reel to ready myself so, once I got the command, I could cast in the direction of what we hoped would be a school of redfish.

"Ready?" the guide asked as he quieted the engine and turned on the trolling motor so we could keep steady despite the current.

"Yep!"

"Go ahead and cast. About 50 yards to the right." He was watching the churn of the water, tracking movement that indicated a transitory school of fish was indeed present.

"I told you there was something here!" Kendyl exclaimed, vindicated, as I threw the weighted fly towards the water. As the fly was bearing down towards the current, I pulled my right arm up sharply, sending the bug back into the air behind me, without it ever touching the water. I repeated this motion a few more times, letting out line and increasing the casting distance with each movement. When I finally had the placement I desired, I let the fly land with a loud thud, about 50 yards off the starboard side of the boat.

Waiting a beat to let the bug sink deeper into the water column, I pulled the line towards me, using a variety of long and short, fast and slow motions to imitate the baitfish's movement that the fly was meant to mimic. I kept my line tight, waiting for any indication that a fish had struck.

But there was nothing. The line remained silent and, as the fly made it back into my casting zone, I sent it sailing again, a few feet to the left of where it had landed the first time.

Again, I started stripping and that's when I felt the tug. It was different from the one I'd experienced in the Texas Hill Country when I was trout fishing. This connection was sudden. Powerful. And left no question in my mind that I was in for a fight.

As I gathered my senses, I pulled the fly line hard to set the hook, kept the rod tip in the air, and tried to bring as much slack line to the reel so I could transition from stripping to reeling. But my efforts were futile because the fly line flew off the reel as the hooked fish changed direction and dove down deep. The line was trying to catch up with the reckless and sporadic movement that was happening in the murkiness of those Louisiana waters, and I was trying to catch up with it all.

"Holy shit!" I exclaimed, reeling in the slack as it came, and keeping just enough tension so the fish wouldn't spit the hook or break the line. "This thing is like a dump truck!"

For several minutes, we danced. As it dove, I let out line and then when it changed direction and came back up, I pulled in the line that had become slack. With each iteration, I brought the behemoth monster a little closer to the boat. I still couldn't tell what it was, but it didn't feel like any of the redfish I'd fought before.

"It looked like a shark," Kendyl would later tell me. And, I was glad she hadn't shared that piece of information in the moment, because I likely would have dropped my rod and let the fight end there.

The minutes ticked by, and my arms started to shake from the fish's show of strength. With each upward pull of my fly rod, I could feel the burn in my right bicep and my left forearm, realizing that the equipment I was using was well underpowered for whatever was on the other end of this line.

"Kendyl," I screamed, "I don't know if I can do this!"

"I'm here!" she replied, and I could feel her gentle hands on either side of my legs, ready to grab me in case this monster pulled me in the drink. Her action, a physical and metaphorical representation of what it felt like when my support structure was in place, when my tribe both literally and figuratively had my back, kept me in the game.

"I was thinking to myself," Kendyl later told me, "there's no way she's letting go of this rod. So, I'm just going to hold on to her because I don't want her to go into the ocean."

I pulled. It pulled. And, for what seemed like an eternity, the dance continued.

Just when I thought I'd given all I had to give, just when I was on the precipice of throwing in the towel, I glanced down at my rod arm, noticing the black glittery nail polish and the three beaded bracelets that hung on my wrist. These were friendship bracelets that I'd obtained the day before, from the young Swifties on Bourbon Street. Part of the Taylor Swift experience included trading friendship bracelets, and my friend Wendy had adeptly prepared us by making some Montana-inspired beauties that we could exchange.

As my eyes locked on the forest green one in the middle of the three, the small white letters gleamed in the sunlight. F-E-A-R-L-E-S-S they spelled. It wasn't fancy, but it was perfect.

"AAAARGGGGGG," I let out a guttural yell, feeling the word penetrate my soul.

I pulled up on the rod, tightening the slack and reeled just a little bit harder.

"I'M FUCKING FIFTY!" I screamed into the horizon, pulling again on the rod and encouraging the fish to come closer to the boat. I could feel my Warrior Woman energy arising, and I knew this was my time. "I'M FUCKING FIFTY," I repeated, "AND I'M FEARLESS!" My scream reverberated off the boat's nonskid deck, off the peaks of the miniature waves that gathered below the hull and bounced into the abyss with power and purpose.

As I stood on the foredeck, unconcerned at how stupid, or downright crazy I might sound to anyone on or off that little boat, I garnered the physical and mental strength to cross the finish line.

"It was the most brilliant thing I've ever heard," Kendyl would later recount. "I couldn't stop laughing. But then again, I was afraid you were going to fall off the boat. So, I was trying not to laugh, but it was just such an exceptional moment."

With a few more concerted tugs and some line management, I finally landed a 35(ish)-pound yellowtail amberjack. These beautiful golden fish are known for their raw power, and they dive deep, looking for shelter in wrecks or other structures, when they feel threatened. As the amberjack arose from the water, I admired its golden scales and the yellowness of its bright anal fin. Despite the incident with the paper gown seven years prior, yellow remained my favorite color. I viewed it, and still consider it, as a color of joy, warmth, optimism, wisdom and energy. And that's the gift this dance had given me.

In New Zealand, the yellowtail amberjack, known as Haku, is a traditional food of the Māori people, and is associated with the qualities of warriors and leaders. In that moment, I felt like both. This beautiful animal was so heavy that I couldn't hold it for a photo. So, our guide held up the tail, while I cradled its head and underbelly, and Kendyl snapped a quick picture. I didn't want to keep the fish out of water too long, because the fight had been exhausting enough and I knew that every second counts in the catch-and-release game.

Thanking my birthday fish and showering it with gratitude for showcasing what it looks like to tap into my own strength, determination and fearlessness, I released it back into the wild with profound appreciation for all it taught me.

"You know Sue," the guide said, as we cleaned ourselves up and prepared to head back to the marina, "I've had guys on this boat twice your size who wouldn't have landed this fish."

I couldn't tell if he was impressed, or downright scared because of the raw, passionate expression of self he'd just witnessed. This is what I wanted my next chapter to look like. Determined. Authentic. Fearless.

"You can be everything you want to be; you just can't be all of it at the same time," Kendyl reminded me. "And, in that, I think it's important to be authentic, because the act of authenticity will bring you organically to where you're meant to be."

I smiled as I reached into my pocket and pulled out another friendship bracelet. I offered it to our guide, with an air of certainty that he wouldn't wear it much after he dropped us off at the marina. That didn't matter. "To commemorate this moment," I said, and then released my grip.

I was learning that sometimes I needed to be the *Gentle Fucking Flower*. Other times, called for me to be the *Battle Axe*. And, sometimes, I needed to show up as both.

Almost exactly a year after that fishing trip, as I was coming up on my eighth soberversary, the universe conspired to gift me another exploratory opening. This time, I was being prodded to dive a little deeper into the authentic vision of my future self. But it was about more than just considering my next chapter. It was about getting crystal clear on the tangible steps I would need to take to make change a reality so I could show up as I had with the yellowtail amberjack - authentically, fearless, and determined.

The federal government had shut down, and I was furloughed. But, instead of worrying about when things would open back up, I used every single day to play with what it would look like to position ideas into actions. Pages of this manuscript came to life, and I had focused conversations about ways I could expand the *Two Gals and a Boat* fly fishing business to incorporate writing circles, workshops and retreats.

Furlough gave me freedom from the 40-hour work week, and I appreciated being able to schedule my days according to the desires of my heart's purpose. I decided to go to New York for a writing conference, and, during the week, we were invited to consider the words we wanted to see on the back of our book jackets.

Writing this future version of myself felt silly, a little brazen even. But it all boiled down to legacy. I thought about the future version of self who would be running retreats and workshops. The Sue who had published her books and who had stood on stages, unafraid, sharing her story and helping other women lift their voices. The Warrior Woman version of myself, who had pushed past the fear and been brave enough to do the things anyway. The gal who trusted in the glimmers and knew God was going to point her in the right direction and provide whatever was needed to fulfill her purpose. As long as I was willing to say yes, I knew my legacy meant owning what was mine to own and not being afraid to step into roles that challenged and stretched me. Future me acted daringly not only in the big asks, but, more importantly, in life's everyday moments.

I looked at the little white notebook in my hands and began to craft my future story.

Dr. Sue Kerver is the founder and CEO of the Sondering Starfish, a multi-faceted approach to combatting the physical and mental health effects of transitions, burnout and stress through narrative healing, ecotherapy and trauma-informed consultation.

She is a New York Times bestselling author, a TEDx speaker, and a Nobel Prize laureate, who is eradicating gender disparity and eco-grief through global research, conservation-focused retreats, and her work with women across the world.

As I read my bio back out loud, I was embarrassed by my own audacity.

"*Nobel Peace Prize? Seriously?*" I asked myself.

"*Yes, Sue, seriously,*" my Warrior Woman countered. "*Somebody is going to do it. Why not you?*"

That was a good question. Why not me?

So, I plugged my future bio into ChatGPT and asked it to create a list of tangible steps that I would need to take to make these ideas a reality. I was looking for both short-term and longer-term actions that would provide some clarity and direction. With a few tweaks, I had a roadmap that I could follow as I continued to navigate the uncertain, yet utterly thrilling, adventure of life. And, the first step was researching graduate schools, to investigate the PhD programs which would allow me to research a body of work that felt inspiring.

"Josh," I said one evening, mid-shutdown, after I'd returned home from New York and spent the day on a series of coaching calls that had truly sparked joy. "There's going to come a day very soon when I will need to step into a different field of work full time. And, when that happens, I want to know that I have your full support."

I waited for him to tell me that my wants don't usurp our needs, that I should be practical and figure out a way to continue to balance my federal position with the work that was defining my future self.

Instead, Josh said, "I have faith in you, Sue. I know you can do it. We'll have to budget, and make some sacrifices, but, together, we will make it work. I would rather see you happy and moving forward than struggling."

I smiled at him, as he added, "We'll get through this together. We always do."

The Sondering Starfish

"What lies behind you and what lies in front of you pales in comparison to what lies inside of you."
- Ralph Waldo Emerson

I'd learned of the concept of Sonder during our first in-person advanced leadership residency in West Virginia, just before shutdowns, Forks in the Road and the requisite Five Bullets decimated the landscape. Doug, one of my colleagues, brought it to our attention as we gathered for our closing ALDP group discussion. We were dancing around the right words to express what it would look and feel like to, over our next year together, create a community that was interconnected but remained open to individual thought and welcomed a space where we could show up, without judgment, bringing all parts of our uniqueness and selves.

"You know," he said, quite astutely, "there's a word for that."

We all looked at Doug, our collective eyes trained on him as we waited for his explanation.

"Sonder," he said, quite matter-of-factly. "John Koenig coined the word when he published *The Dictionary of Obscure Sorrows*. He said that, while we all are the main character in our lives, there are a whole bunch of stories happening within the lives of everyone we actively or passively encounter. So, sometimes we aren't the main character. For someone else, we could be just an extra in the background."

But, for all of the stories to work, everyone matters because we all play different roles, depending on the narrative and point of view.

"This idea of moving from our own stories into the stories of others is so important because connection happens when we understand where we fit into each other's lives!" I thought, letting the word sonder roll around in my head. *"But we can't understand the extent of our role unless people give us a peek into their complex and vivid lives. So, if we don't express our truth, we lose out on the opportunity to fully embrace sonder."*

There is a huge difference between knowing your truth, sharing your truth and living your truth. I didn't share my truth for a long time, partly because I was concerned about judgement, and partly because I wasn't sure anyone would care. What I've come to understand, throughout this journey, is that, when I finally reclaimed my voice, and used it to speak life into myself and others, profound connection happened.

While I was recording *Two Gals and a Mic*, the women who agreed to show up as guests offered their stories as a reminder that connection matters. Sharing ideas, experiences and wisdom provides a conduit for love and levity to manifest because when we own our story, we own our path. And when we own our path, we can help others do the same.

My friend Wendy's decision to share her truth, first in an intimate setting, then later on the podcast, is an incredibly powerful example of what happens when story, positioned as a healing device, offers a pathway forward.

I hadn't met Wendy until I moved to Montana and she expressed interest in fly fishing. I'd connected her with the Bozeman *Project Healing Waters* fly fishing community, and through that, we'd been invited to attend a retreat in Hamilton, Montana – the same one where I'd first met Kendyl. Wendy and I shared a cabin with two other women and, on the second morning, the four of us sat out on the deck, sipped our coffee and watched the birds flitter through the treetops. We recounted our time on the river the day before and wondered how the hours in front of us would unfold.

This retreat offered Wendy her foray into fly fishing, and our little sisterhood celebrated the first ever cutthroat trout that she'd caught the previous afternoon. Then, without any reason except the magic that seems to happen when women gather in quiet outdoor spaces, something incredibly powerful happened on that porch, in between sips of java.

"I want to share something with you," Wendy said as we turned our attention her way. "Something I haven't shared with anyone for 25 years."

I took a long draw of my coffee, hearing a distant "Ok" from across the porch. We were locked in, ready to receive whatever Wendy needed, and wanted, to offer.

"During my time in the Army," she began, as the quiet breeze whispered through the treetops, "I had several instances of military sexual trauma. Those often go unreported for a variety of reasons."

This wasn't the conversation I was expecting to have this morning, and sucked in the crisp, damp air, solidifying that it was, indeed, still early April. The day could unfold with anything from bright sunshine to snowflakes, depending on Montana's mood.

"The last instance of sexual trauma resulted in the pregnancy with my oldest child. I was a single soldier in Belgium. So, imagine being in a foreign country, at 19 years old, trying to sort out how to deal with all this stuff."

I briefly turned my attention to a young doe, which sauntered across the small yard in front of the cabin. In this heavy and emotional tale that Wendy was bravely recounting, the four-legged forest creature became a symbol of hope, of light, of movement.

"The person who did my lab test took me to the train station so that I could go get the pregnancy taken care of," Wendy continued. "I sat at the train station, and I cried the whole day until they came back and picked me up. I knew that I couldn't simply 'take care' of the pregnancy the way they intended. Instead, it resulted in the birth of my son, and I will never regret that decision. But it was life changing. Totally life altering. I was 20 years old, with a baby and I'm in the Army. You get six weeks off after you have a kid, and there I was, a new mom, struggling with the PTSD from the rape."

"What did you do?" one of the front porch ladies asked.

She turned her body to face her and said simply, "Survive."

Survival meant continuing to push forward when Wendy's circumstances and loss of safety were unbearable. Survival meant shoving everything down and compartmentalizing the trauma. Survival meant raising a child, while she carried an unspoken story of grief, pain and loss of agency for over two decades. This was her reality which, as I had come to know from my time with Karen, was not unusual for military sexual trauma survivors.

"Nobody knows," Wendy breathed thinly as the morning air swept away her words. "I've never told a soul. Not a soul."

"Wait," I interrupted, confused with that admission. "What do you mean nobody knows? What about your ex-husband?"

"He doesn't know that all of that stuff had happened."

"What about your son?" I asked. "Does he know?"

"Nobody knows," Wendy repeated as she stared towards the

mountainous horizon. "My ex-husband took care of me after my son's birth, so he believes he is my son's biological father."

"Holy shit," I breathed lightly, as the impact of that statement hit me. "*How does somebody hold that deep of a secret, and live alone in that pain and grief for so long?*" I thought to myself.

We sat in silence for a beat as the impact of Wendy's story hit us.

"Oh Wendy," I finally said, understanding the enormity of this moment. My eyes were blurred with tears as I connected with her pain, and the formidable courage it took for her to release her truth. There was no judgement. No pretense. Just four women, holding a safe space, silently acknowledging this enormously powerful and liberating moment.

"I can't carry it anymore," Wendy stated matter-of-factly. "Twenty-five years of carrying the burden on your own is too long. It takes a toll emotionally and physically. I need to freely let go of this guilt and shame and these hard, heart wrenching feelings." She stared at us, and then again at the mountains in the distance. "I don't need them anymore," she whispered. "They're not serving me."

"*Light always outshines the darkness,*" I thought.

On the *Two Gals and a Mic* podcast the following year, Wendy shared what happened after we left that safe haven.

"A major shift happened there in Hamilton, about what it meant to take my life back by speaking my story out loud. Everything changed. If I've learned nothing else, it's that holding onto those types of things doesn't serve us at all. When you gals allowed me the chance to share my most vulnerable truth, I was given back power over my past, present and future. And the worst-case scenario that I thought was going to happen, when I told the ones I loved, the ones that I had been keeping this secret from for 25 years, didn't happen."

"What did your son say?" I asked.

"He was like, 'Mom, why didn't you tell me? I'm really sorry you had to go through all this stuff by yourself.'"

"And your ex-husband?" I probed.

"The first words out of his mouth were, 'I'm so sorry you had to go through this by yourself.' And I just burst into tears. It was literally the most compassionate thing I could have heard at the time. If he hadn't taken it that way, I don't know that I'd be able to be talking about it again now, on this podcast, because there is a lot of shame involved. But I realize now my silence was the survival mechanism of a 19-year-old who had been raped. I didn't know what else to do."

As Wendy demonstrated, sometimes truth remains hidden not because one lacks the knowledge of how to weave words, images, and narratives together, but because of the shame, guilt and fear that comes with not having a safety net to catch us when we choose vulnerability over remaining stuck.

It wasn't until Dakota, an artisan I met through a women's entrepreneurial group, and I sat and had a cup of coffee in early 2024, that I started to consider what that safety net could, and should, look like.

"How *do* I tell my story?" Dakota asked as she picked up her steaming mug of frothy goodness. Before I could answer, she followed her question with an explanation as to why she wanted to know.

"In my work, I find this really magical place where I get to learn a little bit about the individual and their story and then weave in some of that symbolism to the piece of furniture I'm creating. It becomes a physical manifestation of who they are and who they want to be. But I don't know how to share that."

Storytelling had always come naturally to me, and I did it well in a professional setting. I looked at Dakota as I considered what it might look like for me to break down years of public affairs and communication knowledge into bite-sized, consumable pieces that would not only be applicable for entrepreneurs, but also for people in transition, and those who, like Wendy, were seeking healing.

Her one seminal question became the impetus for me to lay the groundwork so I could effectively help others get in the arena. "*What would it look like,*" I wondered, "*to create a simplified process that would help people through the art of storytelling?*"

I'd spent years in media relations, so I started with my own low-hanging fruit. "What if I offer a workshop on how to pitch a story to the press?" I asked her.

"That could be helpful," Dakota said as she opened her notebook to continue the conversation. "What other ideas do you have?"

As a talented creator, Dakota's Zone of Genius lies in repurposing materials and turning things that no longer have usefulness into valuable pieces with story and function.

Zone of Genius.

I'd first heard that term used when Amanda and I chatted about Sky Oro, an entrepreneurial group that she co-founded in Bozeman to help women experience powerful connections.

"Ask yourself, what lights you up?" Amanda had said, when I asked her to clarify what she meant by that term. "What are you wanting to put out into the world? Once you know that, think about ways that you could spend more time there. Focus five or ten percent more on what you do really well. Because, if we're honest about the short time we have on this earth, we [need to] spend it in our God-given talents versus trying to be good at something that we're not designed to do well."

After that coffee shop conversation, Josh and I commissioned Dakota to revive our dining room table, which was rich with my history, but did not include any of his. Together, we wanted to create a functional piece of art that would tell our collective story, and Dakota was exactly the person who could bring our vision to life.

I originally purchased the dining room table, with two accompanying benches, when I was in the Coast Guard stationed in Guam. Its roughly hewn ebony wood was sourced from Bali, with homemade nails and bits of tar holding the heavy pieces together. Segments of my history were embedded in the now noticeable cracks, which had happened over the journey that the table and I had taken together for nearly two decades. When I'd first bought the family-sized piece, the browns and blacks of the ebony wood melded together and shone as a masterpiece of the wood's exquisiteness. The table's topside gave me space for breaking bread with friends and family, while the two simple legs provided the stoutness needed to keep the piece upright and stable. The two benches, which resembled tree trunks, offered space for everyone to sit comfortably when we gathered to laugh, to cry, to celebrate and to mourn, and for all the other in-between moments that create a colorful life. But, as the years passed, and the table and benches traveled over oceans and across state lines, the ebony lost its shine, the set became lackluster, and time, varied climates and overuse had resulted in its demise.

As I stood in my kitchen in Montana, I pushed slightly on the corner, feeling the table's unsteady legs wobble beneath its warped top piece. Once so strong, so proud, so noble, my heart ached to see this formative piece of furniture so haggard and worn. The table leaned to one side, it's weathered, weak body broken, unsure of its propensity to remain upright and standing on its own. I remembered what it felt like to lose my footing and question my stability. I worried that, if I didn't find a way to bring life back into this piece that had given me so much, it would eventually be declared useless and suffer a tragic, ill-fated ending.

Before moving to Montana, I tried unsuccessfully to sell the set through online platforms, consignment shops and even a garage sale or two. But, as my grandmother used to say, "What's for you will not go by you," and I came to understand that this gathering place, a physical representation of my own wild journey, was meant to stay with me for my second half.

In following the glimmers, I had found restoration and revival out West, and I hoped I could provide the same for this legacy piece. I wanted to see it once again dignified and defined. Like my own battle-tested heart, this table just needed a little love, a second chance, and someone to put it back together as a reclaimed version of itself.

I'd seen river tables, made with live edge slabs, meant to replicate elegant bodies of water. These pieces created the illusion of flow through colorful epoxy and the thoughtful placement of elements collected from the earth's landscapes. Over the course of our first two summers together, Josh and I gathered rocks during our wayward river adventures and dug crystals from a place that had afforded seekers access to these healing elements for the better part of a century. As we amassed these symbols of our time together, Josh and I also formed a foundation for our relationship that felt as solid as the hardness of these natural materials.

The accumulation of Mother Nature's treasures was purposeful, as Josh and I thought that one day we would take the time to repurpose the once-beautiful dining room table into something not only useful and functional, but symbolic of the journey we were on together.

"Part of the creative process," Dakota told us, "is just that courage to explore the unknown, the willingness to try and the belief that something beautiful will emerge."

I appreciated a good creative process, but, more than that, I loved the deeply entrenched stories this piece of furniture held. We endeavored to rework what no longer was useful into something that, at its core, still held the stories of my past, but gave us more runway to tell our collective story of the future. Josh and I wanted to see the possibilities and potential of what the table could become, and I adored the thought of creating new stories once the table regained its footing. And we chose Dakota to help us because she not only had the technical and creative expertise to make our vision a reality, but she had a warmth that invited us into the process.

As we worked with Dakota on the artistic and utilitarian elements, a visual representation of our lived experience started to take shape. We had chosen a section of the Missouri River that was special to us, and asked Dakota to replicate its unique twists and bends. With precision and care, Dakota cut the ragged, aging tabletop into three separate pieces and then planed out the roughness to create a smooth surface.

"Why don't you come by the shop this week," she offered, "to take a look and ensure that everything looks just right?"

Josh and I spent an evening in her workshop, pencils in hand, making intricate marks to areas on the tabletop to note the tiniest of changes. In some places, we made the river's bend a little wider, and in other places, an embankment became a little steeper.

"This is how functional art comes to life," Dakota shared. "The client gets to tell the story of the piece and the creation of it."

When Dakota secured the cut wood in place with metal clamps and ensured we had made all of our desired changes to the riverbanks, Josh and I visited her workshop again, placing the rocks and crystals we'd lovingly collected along the river bottom.

"If you want," Dakota graciously offered again, "you can help with the epoxy. We will pour it and then you can paint each rock and crystal to ensure these pieces remain in place."

I loved that we kept parts of my history and merged those parts with pieces that Josh and I had found together. Dakota afforded us the opportunity to take something old and broken and fashion it into a sturdy, down-to-earth, beautiful piece of art that we could use and enjoy. And assisting in even the littlest of ways created an ownership over the physical manifestation of the life that Josh and I were forming together.

"What is beautiful," Dakota said, "is being able to tap into those sentimental things that are important to people. Sometimes magic happens and something even better emerges than you had originally thought of."

The table became a representation of the love that Josh and I found, without needing to completely erase the history that came before. It was a merger of our stories, and a way to reclaim magnificence in what became more than a simple piece of furniture.

Dakota is a master at telling story through art, but her question about how she could best relay this with wider audiences still gnawed at me. I wanted to come up with a more complete answer than just offering a media-pitching workshop. It took some time, but I let my own creative process emerge because, I knew that there was more to her seemingly simple question and that more deserved an answer.

The idea that profound healing happens when we can connect through story and, in the essence of sonder, understand how we fit into a larger picture, became my own functional art, and the foundation for my next steps. As I began to piece together what I wanted my second half to entail, I decided to pursue a trauma-informed coaching credential through the International Coaching Federation. I launched my coaching practice, became a Wild Writing teacher and I applied, and was accepted to, a graduate program to pursue a PhD in Organizational Development and Change. I saw my federal family drowning in the uncertainty that Five Bullets and Forks in the Road created, so the idea of using my lived experience to help people through these transitions felt truly in alignment with my soul's purpose.

As I thought about Dakota's question of how one might share a story, I thought more about how to integrate storytelling into the coaching, Wild Writing and fly fishing aspects of my work. I wanted to become a leader in integrating these areas and practices.

In the *Warriors and Quiet Waters* "Built for More" program, which I'd completed at the end of 2024, one of the final assignments was to write a letter where I could explore my leadership philosophy. This soulful reflection became an anchor piece for me, because it helped bring all of the treasures I'd collected along my healing journey together into one succinct place.

I've thought a lot about leadership, about purpose, about what these things mean and what it's all supposed to look like. That question I asked myself - and of others – regularly: "What legacy do you want to leave?"

As I move into this next chapter, into my second half, the time for contemplation is being quickly usurped by the need for action. It's time to fully embrace thriving and accept that we are made to live big, because we are gifted with talents, passions, and internal knowings that provide our North Star.

I live by the motto - "Don't die with your song still in you." My Song, my Reason, is a cacophony of all of my experiences, my battles, my hard-earned successes building to a crescendo. And it's leaving room for the unknown notes that have yet to be written.

A life that is full of spirit, sound, vibration, and harmony is a life well lived. I have an obligation - but even more so - a desire, to help others find, and sing, their songs. We all do.

That is leadership.

The Sabotaging Asshat

"If you are going to make a change, it starts with you saying, 'I'm worth it'."
- Brandon Burchard

Rumination - that unwelcomed visitor that appears at the most inopportune times and begs to stay for far too long, playing, performing, and cajoling rent-free in my head. Often, rumination comes disguised as my inner critic, only interested in creating more confusing and self-defeating behaviors to keep me from moving forward. The Sabotaging Asshat who has told me, all my life, that I'm not worthy and that I'll never be good enough to deserve a seat at the table. This little bitch has been planting seeds of doubt and concern for half a century, and I finally decided I'd had enough.

For years, I let my fears and false assumptions dictate my experience instead of challenging my own internal narrative and creating actions to advance my storyline in a way that felt nurturing and authentic. Those years turned into decades where I believed the hidden assumptions that told me I would never be normal, and, because of multiple divorces, a hospitalization, alcoholism, sexual trauma and gender disparity, I would forever be adrift. I had lost jobs. I had lost parents. I had lost faith in myself. And my own negative biases shackled me into believing that I was too broken, and too unlovable, to ever reach my full potential. However, there was no factual data backing up these assertions. I just blindly believed the false narratives because that's what I had spent years telling myself, based on *my* perceptions of what others thought about me.

Our brains are wired to create pathways which associate thoughts with experiences. Those pathways can either connect negative bias with our experiences or connect positive thoughts with the same experiences. For people like me, with complex trauma, connecting to positive biases takes some rewiring, and that work is not for the faint of heart. I spent countless hours working with mental health practitioners using Cognitive Behavior Therapy (CBT) to try and tame my Sabotaging Asshat. I read oodles of books about worthiness, encouragement, manifestation and positive self-talk, rooting around in the darkest corners of my soul to explore how my negative beliefs materialized as somatic experiences or disruptions in my life. I sought out wellness practitioners, spiritual advisors and mentors but still could not release those last sticky beliefs, systems and structures that were keeping me from moving forward.

So, when I got connected with a counselor in Bozeman who paired Eye Movement Desensitization and Reprocessing (EMDR) therapy with fly fishing, my whole world, and some of those stubborn pathways, finally transformed.

"Why are you afraid to step into the spotlight?" she asked me one afternoon as we stood in the river and chatted about my reluctance to publish this book.

I could feel the gentle current flowing past as I invited myself to lean in and see where today's therapy session took us.

I cast my floating grasshopper fly upriver. "I don't know," I answered. Even though I did.

She tried again. "Why are you so afraid to put yourself up on that pedestal?"

I cast the yellow bug again, watching its white, fuzzy wings dance along the current.

"You know," I said, "I've always been the one behind the curtain. I'm the one who makes things happen for everyone else. My entire career has been built on providing support and expertise so other people could successfully be in the spotlight. It just feels odd that, if I publish this book, it'll be me who steps in front of that curtain."

And that's when I felt the weight of what all of it really meant. The reality that putting my voice, my story, and my words out for anyone to read meant I was putting myself out there for criticism as well. People would contemplate. And consider. And some would judge. And that felt terrifying.

The grasshopper floated past again and I mended my line, flicking the weighted, colorful portion upriver. My action was more out of habit than intentionality. I wasn't really fishing. I was just processing. So, the placement of my line didn't matter all that much.

"And what would it look like to switch roles? To step out in front of that curtain?" my counselor asked, watching me as I watched the bug.

I cast again and inspected the terrestrial as it lazily floated by. I thought about all the times I'd been led to do things I didn't feel equipped, or worthy enough to do. This was no different, so why was I so hellbent on trying to find an excuse that would keep me from stepping into my Zone of Genius?

I remembered Amanda's great advice about spending time in our God-given talents instead of trying to be good at something that we're not designed to do well. Nothing about the last two years, about unhinged Executive Orders, nonstrategic government downsizing, and staying in the game to punch the clock felt good.

"*What is it that lights me up?*" I asked myself as I cast my line again, this time a little farther upstream. Instinctively, I knew my answer involved things that would require a spotlight.

I had no doubt God designed me to write, to speak, to create safe spaces for women to share their experiences. And it all started with my willingness to share my story. But all of that felt utterly petrifying and my Sabotaging Asshat told me I would never be worthy enough to do it.

I brought my attention back to the river. My eyes locked on that little, yellow grasshopper that was in the process of transitioning from softer water into the steady churn and chop that arose from a constantly changing riverbed. As it piloted the different sections of the tributary, its little foamy body remained unbothered by the series of large boulders and churning white water that threatened to pull it under.

"Stepping out in front of that curtain feels scary," I admitted to my counselor, who had been standing by the riverbank, waiting for me to answer. "I'm worried. Worried that my story won't resonate. Or that the writing isn't good enough. Worried that my words are too raw or that I'm being too vulnerable. I'm worried that my efforts in putting this out to whomever decides to read it simply isn't enough."

I looked down at my feet. They were sturdily anchored to the riverbed, planted in between the rocks covering the river's sandy bottom. Solid, unflinching.

But that sturdiness came over time, after learning *how* to stand in a river with confidence.

"And, who's opinion really matters?" she countered.

I paused, wanting to skate by with the easy "I don't know" response, but recognized that this topic was important enough to warrant deeper thought and an honest answer.

"*WHO is this really for?*" I asked myself as my left foot shifted slightly in an effort to ground even further down into the riverbed. I thought about my declaration to advocate for other female veterans and I considered what I stood to lose by not following this path, and what I stood to gain by continuing to lean into it.

"What if I'm not remembering my trauma correctly?" I asked her. "I mean, that time on the boat. With the grinning goon. How do I know if that's even real?" I thought about how disgusting and defiled I'd felt after facing off with the toothy- grinned troll, because there was no space in the military, or even afterwards as I stepped into leadership positions, to share stories of these types of encounters.

I stopped casting and looked at my counselor. "What if I'm making this whole thing up?" The tears came again. I didn't feel like I was making anything up, but I had been gaslighted and questioned so many times, I just wasn't sure.

"That's not how trauma works, Sue."

I stared at her, waiting for her to explain how it does work.

"Your brain holds onto traumatic experiences in a different way than regular memories," she said. "It remembers these experiences in fragments, instead of in coherent narratives. Which is why it can be hard to piece things together. But, even if that's not exactly what happened, there is something there that your brain is associating with a traumatic event. And, a lot of times, that association happens because of a sensory stimulant."

I considered the olfactory evidence that seemed to trigger me.

"*Huh,*" I thought to myself as I mentally went through the rolodex of smells that often enticed a physical reaction. *Magnolias in bloom. Hospitals. Cigarette smoke. Decaying fish. Salt air. Green grass.* The reactions weren't always negative, but these smells were powerful reminders of places I'd been and experiences I'd had.

"So then, something did happen?" I asked. "You know. On the boat that day?"

"Most likely," she said.

I picked up my fly rod and cast again.

Something had to have happened. An egregious story like that wouldn't have simply come from my imagination. And, even if I wasn't crystal clear on the details, the series of events had to have been heinous enough for my mind to want to catalog them as a disorganized group of snapshots instead of safely storing them as a whole narrative memory. Piecing those events together with cohesiveness, especially when, before TMS, my pre-frontal cortex was not at peak performance and unable to retrieve and organize these fragments in any sort of congruent way, made it even harder to want to share my story.

"I'm worried that once I put my story out, there are going to be people who will tell me my experiences weren't as significant as theirs, or will want to debate the merits of my MST or PTSD. They'll tell me my writing sucks or whatever other myriad of things they can find to pick apart."

I had already been through that gauntlet once before, when I was on a fly fishing retreat with mixed company. As I shared some of my experiences in the Coast Guard, I was told that the resulting PTSD didn't merit the same consideration as the issues that my combat veteran brothers and sisters were struggling with. This unsolicited feedback infuriated me. I was so tired of men telling me that my story didn't matter. And, that Sabotaging Asshat is a wily devil.

"There probably will be people who do that and say those types of things," my counselor acknowledged. "So, you have to have your foundation in place to make sure you can weather the storm."

I paused, looking around at the smattering of trees that lined the embankment. I looked up at the cloudless sky, and back at the water, a steady stream that continued to move despite storms, seasons, or situations. My foundation, which I'd built from eight years of hard work. Habits of self-care, positive narratives that aligned with my truest identity, a strong support structure, my faith, and purpose that had arisen from the ashes, when I realized that my story did indeed matter. This book was more than a glimmer. It became my gift.

Many times, throughout the process of writing it, as I spent late nights culling through my memories and squaring off with all the doubt and uncertainty, I asked myself a simple question. *"Is it worth all this?"*

My friend Jamicka, an Army veteran and accomplished marathon runner, helped me answer this question. "A lot of people make me feel like I don't matter," she had once said. "But there are so many more people in my life that make me feel like I do. Everyone has a purpose. As long as we have breath, we matter."

And, despite the Sabotaging Asshat, or the objectors who had, and likely would, tell me my story, my words, my writing didn't matter, I knew my efforts were worth the fight.

"Somewhere," I said to my counselor, "someone needs to hear that she matters. She needs to know that she's not alone and, even in the darkest of places, there really is hope." I inhaled sharply, using my breath to suck down the emotional torrent that was threatening to breach my own waterline. "I really wish someone had been there to tell me these things eight years ago. Maybe then the journey wouldn't have been so rocky."

It was difficult to accept that there would be people who would never understand my words, or my offerings. But it was more important to recognize that there would be those who would read them and see themselves in the pages, the paragraphs, the simple sentences. And it was my hope that, when this happened, they would understand that healing is possible. They would know that they are not alone and that their lives, and what they do with their time here on earth, matters greatly.

On that river, with the steady flow of snowmelt beneath my feet, re-anchoring to my why felt necessary. There was no more space for questioning. It was time to unleash my Warrior Woman and kick that Sabotaging Asshat to the curb. It was time to take my curtain call.

Be The Starfish

"When you become uncomfortable with uncertainty, indefinite possibilities open up in your life."
- Eckhart Tolle

As I look back on my journey, I recognize that there was no guidebook, no process, no checklist that anyone could have provided which would have made walking my path any easier. Each rock I turned over, each question I asked, each answer I pursued, and each story offered by a fellow Warrior Women afforded me the pieces of the puzzle that I needed so I could piece together a beautiful mosaic that is now my lived experience.

In the eight years of moving from surviving to thriving, I recognized that my own propensity to push forward was directly correlated to how much protection, order and direction I could create. I needed a way to organize my thoughts, my actions and my next steps and, when there was no structure, I created my own scaffolding which allowed me to feel solid and stable, even when everything around me was shifting. This is how I operated in the gray.

As I moved through the complexities of 2025, operating in the gray became my new normal. So, I created even more protection, order and direction by amalgamating the lessons I learned and designing a framework to bring calm to the chaos.

In developing this framework, I kept coming back to the starfish. On the surface, these colorful creatures provide a variety of shades, textures and marks which make them easy to identify and distinguish from one another. The above-the-surface elements also provide protection, armor, and, at times, camouflage, to keep the starfish safe from predators and other unpredictable circumstances. In the most basic sense, the above-the-surface aspects are the things that are implicit, tacit and easily comprehended. For me, the above-the-surface aspects boil down to four key elements: ***Support***, ***Time***, ***Action*** and ***Reason***. Together, the lessons learned and the experience gathered in these areas became my **STAR** which, like a supernova, provided a way for me to navigate difficult decisions and find clarity that was anchored in evidence, experience and enlightenment.

I also considered the below-the-surface aspects of the starfish - the underbelly - which is the epicenter of mobility, nourishment and life. Under the water is where feet provide movement and stability during tumultuous circumstances. Below the surface is where the starfish eats the mussels and sea urchins that keep it alive. And, below the waterline is where a starfish takes in the nutrients, and the saltwater, it needs to breathe. As I thought about my own journey, the below-the-surface elements which kept me grounded and in alignment were my ***Foundation***, ***Intuition***, ***Strengths*** and ***Habits***. When considered together, these four elements created my **FISH** giving me forward momentum, and allowed me to breathe, even when I felt like I was suffocating or stuck. When considered together, these above and below the surface factors create a whole starfish, which as a keystone species, can produce a rich, vibrant, thriving ecosystem.

Over the years, **Support** showed up in my life in countless, unexpected ways. Sometimes, it was through people - a conversation with Karen or Donna as we walked the dogs, a reflection session on the river, a story or dream shared in the drift boat, or wise words that many women shared on the podcast. As I worked through my transition from victim to victorious, support also appeared as organizations with programs to help me understand myself, resources to address medical and emotional concerns, and experts who helped me navigate the uncharted territory of hope, health and healing.

The life walk in Georgia, the envisioning my future self in New York, and the understanding that sometimes things, like starting a podcast were *yes, but not yet* situations which helped me realize and recognize the importance of patience, trust and **Time**. As I reflect on the last eight years and the incremental healing that's taken place in phases, time was the gift I needed in order to unpack the untruths and let go of the burdens that were weighing me down. Keeping me stuck. It took time to reclaim my voice and reconnect with my Warrior Woman. It took time to learn my intuitive love language so I could follow the glimmers. It took time to cultivate relationships with trusted individuals so I could begin to share my story. And it took an immense amount of time to build up my courage and allow myself to feel joy, fall in love, and truly believe that my life and legacy are worth every brick I've had to carry.

As I rediscovered parts of myself that had lain dormant, hidden, or underutilized for a very long time, I wondered what it would look like if I finally gave myself permission to blend the *Battle Axe* parts of me with the *Gentle Fucking Flower* parts, so my strength, fearlessness and boldness could be in congruence with the compassionate, squishy side of myself. As I took **Action** towards creating this congruency, I allowed myself incremental wins. When I showed up five to ten percent more aligned, or rooted, or grounded, I considered these wins as significant milestones that, in time, had a cumulative and positive effect on my capacity for growth. I put a lot of thought into what I wanted more of in life, what I wanted less of, and what served me well. With careful consideration and intention, I built a business I didn't feel prepared to build, launched a podcast that would expose my vulnerabilities, and, in those actions, I let go of my need for perfection and unrealistic expectations. I allowed myself the grace to explore and to try new things, which gave me the space and capacity to wonder, to be curious and to dream big.

In private conversations with God and with my own Warrior Woman, though written entries in my journal, where I could unashamedly, and without judgement, unpack the messiness of my conscious and unconscious parts, and with every decision to share more of my story, I always anchored in my WHY. At the inception of my healing journey, I wanted to share parts of my story because I wanted to know that I wasn't alone. As my Warrior Woman grew stronger, and I connected with others who were not afraid to share their wisdom and hard-earned knowledge to help light the way, my **Reason** for sharing parts of my healing journey became anchored in a passion for creating safe spaces for people to feel empowered to tell their stories and connect with self, nature and others. Not only did I want to light the path for those coming after me, but I also wanted to create structures, conduits and routes to amplify the collective voice, which would offer the light, hope and love needed to outshine the darkness.

These four elements, ***Support***, ***Time***, ***Action*** and ***Reason***, my ***STAR***, served as my wayward finding compass. It's how I found the courage to advocate for myself and to continue to push forward with the hope of a better tomorrow, even when everything felt murky, unclear and unsettled.

As I dove below-the-surface to examine the deeper parts of myself, I discovered that my **Foundation**, which was comprised of my core values, beliefs and North Star, is what kept me in alignment. During TMS, I did a lot of core value work, and discovered that, when I could move towards living a life that was aligned with my personal values, which included making a lasting contribution to the world; having meaning, direction and purpose in life; sharing personal stories and intimate experiences with others; being genuine and acting in a way that is true and authentic to my whole self; and living a life filled with new and exciting adventures, my anxiety and depression decreased, and my feelings of connectedness and satisfaction soared.

Understanding my foundation also helped me figure out how to reconcile the tension between what I stood to lose (*security, identity, stability*) in making big decisions with what I stood to gain (*alignment, purpose, autonomy*). And this juxtaposition of less versus more, and loss versus gain, became part of my North Star. I boiled my actions down to a few simple questions: *Does this choice or action feel authentic to who I am and who I want to become? Is it in alignment with my values? Does it allow me to fulfill my purpose in this world?* If I could answer those questions with unequivocal "yeses," then I knew I was on the right path.

My foundation also integrated my beliefs, which meant I had to take a hard look at the internal narratives propelling me forward, and the Sabotaging Asshats that were holding me back. A lot of the work involved with letting go of my false beliefs was based in understanding how to share my story. Our stories are our gifts, and not all gifts are meant for all people. By consciously choosing when I needed to share, and how much made sense depending on the environment, circumstances and relevancy, I created psychological safety so I could incrementally build and strengthen my storytelling muscle. The more I experimented with how I wanted to share my truth, and the more I allowed people in, who respected me enough to listen without judgement, the easier it became to start to believe that I was, indeed, worthy, enough, strong, fearless and bold. As I continued to give the gift of my story, I became more selective in what I wanted to give away and what I wanted to keep for myself. My level of transparency fluctuated depending on who I was talking to and how I thought my message would be received. The magic wasn't in the story; it was in being brave enough to tell it in a way that honored my core self. Doing this narrative healing in safe and respectful ways helped me shift my own internal dialogue and change the critical tapes that had played on repeat for decades.

A large part of my healing journey was also couched in **Intuition** and learning to listen to, trust and follow the glimmers that led me home. There was a lot of fear associated with trusting my gut, my heart, and God, instead of solely relying on what my head believed to be true. But, in that surrender, I found that my life unfolded in beautiful ways. Belize is a perfect example. As I look back on the times I said *yes* to the things that didn't fully make sense, but I instinctively knew were right, I can see how the breadcrumbs were laid out in a way that I could follow, without having to know exactly where I was going. The most difficult part about intuition is that it required me to loosen the reins on the responsible, sensible, pragmatic sides of myself, so I could allow expansiveness and possibility to flow, uninhibited, like the rivers that I loved so much. While intuition became an important part of my decision-making strategy, I remained firmly rooted in my faith, in nature, and in seeking advice from my trusted 3-5 inner-circle people. The combination of these factors let me act in accordance with my values instead of fear, and I found solace in knowing that the decisions I made didn't have to be permanent. I had the agency and authority to change my mind if things didn't work out. But, over time, I found that the more aligned my decisions were with my foundation, and with intuition, less and less course correction was required.

My **Strengths** also played an important role in navigating my path forward. When I was at *Camp Southern Ground*'s Warrior Week in Georgia, I completed the Clifton StrengthsFinder test and spent several days diving into how each of my strengths could have positive, or potentially detrimental, effects on my life. Connectedness, Individualization, Belief, Ideation and Arranger showed up as my top five. So, as I moved forward in thinking about the type of work I wanted to do, and the way I would make a lasting contribution through legacy and purpose, I found ways to employ my strengths so they could be instrumental to my success in this next chapter.

I also created **Habits**, which ranged from asking for support when I needed it, to carving out the space and time to do the hard work of healing. My habits included self-care, walks with Meatball, time on the river, hikes in the mountains and grounding myself to the earth, as I'd done when I practiced yoga in the hospital's green grass. I leaned into gratitude, journaling and prayer, so I could create balance between the grind and the gift. And I made time for the people and things I loved, like my husband Josh, whom I absolutely adore, because they were as much a priority as my work or professional aspirations.

The beautiful, and profound, benefits that come from doing this glorious work of healing is that it creates opportunities for growth and hope. But, rebuilding also means relinquishing. We're faced with the choices to adapt, to evolve, and to move with the ebb and flow of life's tidal swings, all while letting go of what no longer serves us. When we do that, and lean into what may inform who we want to become as our future selves, instead of who we have been as the selves stuck in the past, that movement, that momentum *becomes* our story.

When we understand our story, we understand ourselves. And it is in that profound acceptance that we may, as my Warrior Woman advised so many years ago, be the starfish.

The Grace Of Imperfection

"Your cracks can become the most beautiful part of you."
- Candice Kumai

In Japanese culture, "kintsugi" is a traditional repair method that connects broken pieces of a shattered vessel together with thin lines fashioned from gold lacquer, resulting in a new and distinctive vessel. Often, during the last eight years, I thought of myself as that broken vessel but never paused to consider the, "what happens when you piece yourself back together," question. So, when I came across a small, paperback book entitled, "Did I Tell You?" by Elizabeth Knapp, peeking out from in between the hardbacks on my bookshelf, I stopped dead in my tracks.

My mom had gifted me this little gem 34 years ago, and I'd forgotten all about it. For three decades, the book sat dormant on various bookshelves, being moved from place to place, crammed in between bigger, bolder, brighter hardcovers and trade paperbacks. In its silence, this little goldmine, stuffed full of wisdom and knowledge, waited for the day when I was writing this book, and needed to hear the wisdom that lay in those pages.

As I stood in my home office on this chilly Montana morning, my hands flipped through the worn linen pages of that tiny book, noting the whimsical green text interspersed with simplistic, hand-drawn flowers and the pages that were slowly coming unbound from the two tiny staples holding them together.

I started to read the fine cursive, stopping to ponder the

messages about life's meaning, discovery of self, and finding joy and restoration in nature.

I turned the page.

More green cursive script, with passages that spoke to being bold and courageous. These words symbolized all the things my mom should have, could have and would have said to me, if we had had a relationship that afforded that kind of intimacy.

Yet, she didn't.

But ironically, as I read these messages, I realized I had lived a life that embodied all of these things my mom had hoped for me. Even without her direct guidance.

I flipped to the middle section of the tiny book, my eyes stopping on the second part of the verse that was written around a willow, the flower symbolizing humanity.

"Did I tell you," the script said, "to serve other people if only in a small way. There is growth and satisfaction in being part of something larger than yourself and your life will be richer for knowing this."

"*Truth,*" I thought, and kept flipping.

Then I turned to the inside back cover.

Penned in blue ink, Mom's cursive script swept across the yellowing page.

"Did I tell you everything that is worthwhile is hard work"

No punctuation. No fanfare. Just a parting shot from beyond the grave.

"Hard work," I said out loud, noting that Meatball was the only one within earshot.

I let the words roll around on my tongue. Two little words, with so much complexity.

I had spent eight years "doing the hard work" of putting myself and my life back together. I had wrestled with understanding what loss, and then the sweet reconnection with love, voice, agency and purpose felt like. And, through it all, I often wondered if it was in vain, because maybe I was too fragmented, too cracked to be put back together – even through metaphorical kintsugi.

I worried that if I did find a new shape for my vessel, the "new me" would be so profoundly different, and so flawed with my wounds and battle scars, that I wouldn't have any usefulness or value.

The irony is, if I never would have shattered, I never would have had the courage, or even the desire, to seek out and build community. I never would have found voice, purpose, passion and payoff. And I never would have embarked on the Hero's Journey which led me to discover the treasure I had inside of me all along.

I sought an end, a destination, a finish line that I could proudly cross, the same way I had when I completed my Ironman. But what I would come to understand, and something I wish someone had told me, was that there is no finish line. There's simply transformation into the next stage, and then whatever learning comes from that.

Our mistakes, our traumas, our experiences make us into these uniquely beautiful vessels, able to walk through life as a living legacy, embracing the perfectly imperfect and practicing grace and loving acceptance in a world which, ironically, tells us we must be perfect. In healing, there is no perfect. And there certainly is no destination. Instead, there are a whole lot of in-betweens that create the texture and beautiful designs of each of our unique lives. It's the in-betweens that make each and every one of us unique, even with our battle scars.

The beauty that I didn't yet see was that the exploratory process allowed me to recreate my body, my mind, my spirit, using kintsugi, with all my thin gold lines showing up as lessons learned, growth and self-love that I gathered along the way.

As my journey evolved, it became clear that healing really wasn't about fighting through anxiety, depression and post-traumatic stress to get rid of these factors in my life. Because, with trauma, there is no magic bullet to erase what happened and eradicate the parts of self that were affected. Instead, there is healing through the residual disarray that is left after the storm clears, learning how to grow, adopting new ways of thinking, and moving into places where we can thrive.

I couldn't erase any of my past, but I could consider how I wanted it to define my future. And, as much as I ached for resolution, I came to understand that healing is about living with, and not so much living without, the great, and the not-so-great, parts of self. There's no getting rid of anything because all of the messiness of my past, and the ways I had interacted with it, was as much a part of me as whatever my future would hold. But, as I became more curious, tenacious and unrelentless in adapting solutions that felt authentic, and in alignment with the person I wanted to become, I recognized that I could live with anxiety, depression, post-traumatic stress and even moral injury because, while they are part of my fabric, they are not the totality of who I am. There is so much more to me than these diagnoses and I never would have tapped into that incredible, and sacred contract of self, if I hadn't allowed myself to feel, to experience, to move through the depths of the deepest pain and find healing and support along the way.

What I realize now is that I was broken into a million different pieces so I could be restored in a way that was even more beautiful than the original. As I've learned to accept imperfection and impermanence, I've learned to trust the glimmers by leaning into things that don't always make sense. I've felt empowered to put voice to the things I not only need but want. As I move into my second half of life, I can see now that my new vessel, which has been intricately pieced back together, is complete because it is full of beautiful cracks that are highlighted in gold. And it's not flawed. Instead, it's perfect. Perfect because it represents where I've been, how I adapted, but, most importantly, how I evolved into a piece of unique artwork that carries the value of experience, resilience, connectedness and power to live in a way that is authentic to who I am. I have evolved thoughtfully and with intention, so the cracks and imperfections I show are not weaknesses, or shameful embarrassments. They are a compilation of a hard-earned fight that has turned into something beautiful over time. And, I am able to celebrate the unique beauty in all of this, because I recognize the patience and the care that was required to piece it all back together.

Moving from chaos to alignment is not for the faint of heart. Like it or not, we are all playing the long game.

In the TMS chair, my Warrior Woman demanded that I be the starfish. It took a long time for me to fully understand what that meant. Adapting to our circumstances, and then evolving to surpass them by creating ways to thrive, on our own terms, takes time. A starfish generally moves only a few inches per minute, but its movements are strong, deliberate, and intentional. It can hold fast and create a secure grip, even when strong waves and unpredictable environments threaten to sweep it away. It's the journey, not the destination, that makes the process so beautiful.

As you piece your own vessel back together with whatever golden lacquer becomes your glue, relish the ups and downs, the winding roads, the uneven terrain, and the excursions that don't always seem to have a destination. These in-betweens are how you rebuild yourself into the beautiful masterpiece you truly are.

Thank you for taking this journey with me. I wish you peace, blessings and an abundance of wisdom as you find your way and travel your path.

Let's shine together.

About The Author

Sue Kerver is a passionate advocate for service, storytelling, and the empowerment of women, on the water, in leadership, and through life's transitions. A Montana fly fishing guide and instructor, trauma-informed coach, Coast Guard–licensed Captain, and lifelong outdoor enthusiast, Sue draws on both professional expertise and lived experience to help women step into confidence, clarity, and their authentic voices.

She is the founder of **Two Gals and a Boat™**, a fly fishing education platform rooted in conservation, community, and the belief that women belong in outdoor spaces, fully and unapologetically. Sue also hosted the **Two Gals and a Mic** podcast (©2024), where she has interviewed more than fifty extraordinary women, amplifying stories of resilience, courage, and self-discovery.

Sue holds a Master of Business Administration in Leadership from The Citadel and a Master of Communications and Journalism from the University of Georgia. With a background in communications and public relations, she blends strategic insight with a deep love of storytelling to help individuals navigate change, reconnect with purpose, and lead with intention.

Her career includes nearly two decades of federal service, including more than ten years in the U.S. Coast Guard. During her service, Sue worked on the West Coast, East Coast, Gulf Coast, and overseas, responding to natural disasters such as the Deepwater Horizon oil spill and supporting large-scale national events, including President Obama's second inauguration. After leaving the Coast Guard, she continued her service through work with veterans, in agriculture and in wildlife conservation.

Sue also served as a Peace Corps volunteer in Ethiopia, where she taught English and sustainable development. She also spent time crewing on a 40-foot catamaran, building her sea legs and beginning the journey toward earning her Merchant Maritime 100-ton Near Coastal captain's license.

With a unique blend of military service, outdoor leadership, and heartfelt storytelling, Sue is dedicated to helping others uncover their authentic voices and live with confidence, connection, and purpose.

When she isn't writing, fly fishing, skiing, hiking, or camping, Sue can be found soaking up time in nature with her husband, Josh, and their Chocolate Lab, Meatball.

To learn more about working with Sue, view upcoming workshops, and for speaking/event inquiries, visit her website - *www.suekerver.com* - or scan the QR code.

www.ingramcontent.com/pod-product-compliance
Lightning Source LLC
Chambersburg PA
CBHW051506050726
47594CB00010B/3993

* 9 7 8 1 9 6 1 1 8 5 9 4 4 *